KISS MY CROSS

KISS MY CROSS

LYNETTE DUROCHER

This book is dedicated to anyone who has human moments like me. May God make you smile again, encourage you to keep fighting, and may you bring someone else up with you when you come!

Contents

CHAPTER 1

WHY ARE YOU LAUGHING?

Hi, my name is Lynette, and I was born a middle child. I am rambunctious, tenacious, and a bit of a rebel. I have a funny side and I love to joke. Oh, and I forgot to mention that I love JESUS. You heard! I also have an undying love for: art and fashion, music, and comedy. Take this journey with me through this memoir on loving God while being edgy in my memoir *Kiss my Cross*.

My name, Lynette, means pretty one in French. While I consider myself an average to good-looking woman, I have always loved to doll myself up since being a kid. This book isn't about such shallow things, though. It's about the love of laughter and my journey to find God and get back to Him. Yes, I love wine and JESUS and only God can judge right? Watch me as I walk my walk. No wait, sis, you know what I meant was walk with Christ. My life began in 1977 in Long Island, New York. As I lay outside the family house in the Hamptons, we'd enjoy sipping iced tea and watching the dogs run in the yard as the sun set. Yeah, right. The ninth commandment in the Bible says, "Thou shall not lie."

I grew up in a subsidized low-rent apartment and yes in Long Island. The good news is I am out of there now. What I did know was family ties and friendships, attending church three to four times weekly, but I never knew how my life would be today.

My hobby then was taking photos of family members while they were sleeping. I also enjoyed getting lost outside on adventures purposely and torturing my little brother. Before you think badly about me, this was around the time when I was twelve and I had an older sister who was torturing me. So, mind your damn, no (holy rolling) business. You liked that, didn't you? Ok, enough of that, now just read the book.

As a kid I grew up as a poor African American and lived in subsidized housing. I didn't realize then that Black was beautiful, powerful, and resilient. I lived in a community of Black and Brown people in my neighborhood, never fully comprehending other races existed until school. My family had strong faith. This required us to attend church often. At that time, I was expecting some Christian credit like, Jesus, you know I am here again this week.

My school district, thankfully, was a melting pot of races. We had families of White, Black, Hispanic, Asian, and Caribbean descent and gratefully, I was exposed to them all. I love New York! This was a great start for me because I knew that one day, that is what Heaven would look and be like. I learned a great deal about other cultures, but even with that I noticed some of my closest friends were like me. Today, I know this is not ideal because we were created for fellowship. It also is good to intermingle to share our thoughts and perspectives and our differences to learn more about one another. Why? Because the world is vast, duh!

Now let's move on to embracing being Black and beautiful. I was led growing up to many positive role models. Three I can easily name off the top of my head. My oldest sister, childhood friend Brea, and Sister Leanne, the church "Auntie." These ladies embodied what being Black and beautiful meant and it led me on to know that one day I could be this way, too. My sister was gifted and beautiful. She was both curvy and attractive and had a gift for singing. My friend was beautiful. She was lanky and tall, having a body and face like a model. Then there was the church Auntie, and she was a doll. She was gorgeous and classy, with every hair in place as if it was a wig. One day in the ladies' room after choir she told me her hair was "tamed." I wish someone would tame this hair of mine. Three beautiful women from three different generations with one thing obviously in common. They all were Black and all beautiful. Just maybe I had a chance.

Somewhere I found the courage to embody my Blackness and my beauty. Let me start though by saying that my path started a little differently. I was a chubby Black girl from the projects with a wide nose, but this didn't mean I couldn't improve on myself. This would be a big transition, being the youngest female in a family of four older women. Being the youngest female, I was often over talked, ignored, and undervalued. I built a reputation at that time on not taking nonsense by fighting, which I am not proud of today, but went on to build a name for myself in my family. Well, I broke out of my shell, out of my neighborhood, and temporarily out of my family to attend a Historically Black College and University.

So going from a multicultural high school to a Black college was a culture shock for me. I went from eating bagels and cream cheese, hoagies, Chinese meals, and beef patties with cocoa bread to moving to the South. In the South it was ok to eat ramen noodles with Spam. Corned beef hash was a breakfast food and potted meat is of the devil! Understand when I say South, I really wasn't in the deep South. I was in Virginia. I was introduced to the new world of being Black. Now that I was many hours away from home and trying out new food customs, it was time for me to make some changes.

I would start by swearing off God, church, and change. I would embrace my "Black girls rock" mojo and show these people what I was working with! This was a very dumb decision. The Bible does say as I recall, "God takes care of fools and babies." I was eighteen years old at this time and my baby days were long over. I wanted to have the Black college experience of gaining a degree, love, and success. My focus was on studying for my pre-med, soon-to-be physician career and in my free time partying like a rock star. I wanted to experience Black love because why not, friend?

I graduated from attending an HBCU with a bachelor's degree, a baby, and meeting the love of my life. On day one of college, I was undecided on my major and made a split decision in choosing my major. I either wanted to be a fashion designer, business lawyer, or a neurosurgeon. The closest education track my college offered was pre-med, so I chose biology as a major for my undergraduate studies.

Now I was ready and committed to studying the sciences and I didn't mind starting with human anatomy. (Sheesh these young and wild hormones on a campus full of chocolate men will get you in trouble). One, two, three, not it! I am jumping ahead a little, but this was to my disadvantage senior year. I gave up on wanting to pledge sorority, and missed out on graduating on time because I somehow ended up pregnant (Holy, help). To my advantage, I met an amazing guy. Yes, I met many guys, so don't ask. This guy was different, though, in that he intrigued me. His smile was like none I had ever seen before, full of curiosity and promising adventure. I knew two things. I wanted him and I could have him. It was time then to ante up. I had to do the challenging thing and call my parents and break the unwelcome news to them.

What was the news you asked? I got pregnant in my senior year of college in my pre-med undergraduate class. What this meant was that I couldn't enter med school the following year. I would have to decide to either have my baby and stop or take a break from continuing to become a physician. Wait a minute. Easier said than done. I made an executive decision to call my parents eight hours away to tell them I was pregnant and no longer going to become a physician. Did my mom just hang up on me? She did, and she told me that I had to break the news to my father myself and for two months he wouldn't even speak with me. That same year, the father of my child took me into his home with his parent but wouldn't swear off cheating with other women. I realized he didn't want to pursue having a relationship with me, but said he just wanted his baby. What I didn't know then was that I deserved better because I had this fairytale in mind.

My parents offered for me to move back home with my infant baby since her dad ended the relationship. My mom made me an offer then to leave my child home with her and return to college to medical school to continue my pursuit to become a doctor. It was very gracious, and I was grateful for the opportunity to continue my education and career choice, but instead I chose my daughter. That is another story, and in another book, I can give you more insight on that. Side note for those out there who have support, you are blessed and fortunate to use it and once you reach your accomplishment, stay humble.

I realized and quickly that I needed to go back and find God, but first I would find my friend. It was time to muster up the courage to tell him the news, but by now he could see it with his own eyes. A bun was in the oven, and it was my oven. How did I get here, Christ? Well, an HBCU is filled with melanin and so many guys were on campus. There were nerds and jocks, frat boys and hood boys and even present were the "local yocals." (The local yocals were men not in school but of or close to college age that liked to hang out near campuses to pick up young women.) The frat boys were fun for dancing and parties and the locals mostly were idiots. (Whoops, I meant uninteresting.) I dated a DJ for free access to partying and to have something to do when I wasn't studying so hard. Free tip here, everyone. Solely dating for familiarity or comfort isn't always a good thing. I also met a jock, and athletes were always easy on the eyes, but some have been known to be unfaithful. In all honesty, I like the guys that are bigger with the athletic type of build. Unintentionally, I fell for a jock and boy were we different.

Let's talk about the friendship created before I stumbled into parenthood. This guy, my friend, was unbelievable. He was attractive and my classmate, flashy, had a great smile, and was super nice. What was wrong with this guy? I know I was judgmental, right? The New York in me and my strong maternal upbringing made me weary of every smiling man. Close in and listen to this. You can't be led by past hurt when you're moving on in life. All situations are not the same and neither are all people. We do not want to miss out on a good thing because we are sabotaging it before it can even happen.

Hashtag Smiley, let's call him, was young and built. He was a football player and had a big wide chest. But beneath this big exterior was a timid, naïve country boy with a Caribbean background. The heart wants what it wants, right. And my body wanted a sexual encounter with him. I swore I would pray for forgiveness later, OK. Dear God, I know I'm dating this DJ dude, but this smiling guy has piqued my interest.

He's new and shiny and smiles like the Cheshire cat, but wait, his eyes are red. He is nothing like my ideal type. He's wearing a Tommy shirt, flip-flops, and he has an accent! What about the red eyes? He isn't evil, so what is it? Could he be a weed head? I decide to confront him on this, and he tells me he wears contacts, and he has really bad allergies. Oh, thank God! I must get to know him better. My disinterested baby-father-to-be later may get jealous but oh well. WWJD, really, sis?

Music appreciation class was where we met. I made the decision to stick to calling my guy friend Smiley. I found out Smiley and his friends were in a crew known as the "Florida Boys." They mostly were members of our college football team and many of them there at college were on academic scholarships. Later I discovered that about half of these guys were of Caribbean background, so technically they reminded me of episodes of old school shows like *Miami Vice* or *Bad Boys*. If you do not know these shows, close this book and go sit down somewhere. (Hah!) Wait, come back. This is not Christianly behavior from me, my bad. Back to these boys who were athletes by day and party friends by night. We spent our college weekends in the clubs. To my happy discovery I found out Smiley can dance, and I mean really dance, so I have a newly found dance partner.

Now dancing is my middle name and I love to do it. Stella is my actual middle name after my namesake, my grandmother. I wanted to dance, and that I did. I spent my nights percolating and dollar whining and slow dancing with the college boys. Some were potential crushes and prospects, and others were just for the fun of it. I figured nothing was wrong with dancing. After all, didn't King David in the Bible dance? Dancing makes me feel free, as an expression of my essence allows me to truly let go and be lit. This is at least what my inner child tells me. To my surprise, when I offered Smiley a dance and realized he had something extraordinary in him that paired well with me, I couldn't get enough. I mean, the dude really could dance and was one of the first guys of a few that could keep up with my moves then. I will stick a pin right here and re-visit this point. I was so excited to find a man who could match my dancing, energy, and curiosity.

CHAPTER 2

WHEN A COLD SHOWER GETS YOU RIGHT

First stop, heading back to my dorm room for a cold shower first. All this slow grinding has gotten sis hot and bothered. Whew! Please, pardon me, I am back to my senses. Here is where I insert the disclaimer that college is full of a variety of fine, young men, and I wanted to have my fair share of sampling. To reign in these thoughts, I decided to attend my university chapel and local churches from time to time. Chapel was cool. It was a way to connect in a mellow, not overly traditional Christian way. It was informative and by attending I received a certain number of credits towards my graduation. Now, as a young adult college student, I can't tell or promise you how much of the teaching I retained.

My college developed a Bible study club, and I decided to attend. A group of college peers and myself would meet weekly and talk about the Bible and God. It was nice, but I knew they were not going to keep singing that song…LOL. I settled on the idea that it was ok to attend from time to time. No longer, though, was I going to be a religious fanatic like my family. As I got closer to fulfilling my chapel requirement for graduation, I began to slack off. Then I realized that I could take a break from God and church. Boy, was I young and dumb then.

Going forward, I would plan my weekend activities, including dancing in clubs, hanging out with my girls, and dating. I was a science nerd by day and a club slash house party dancer by weekend. One day in my college cafeteria I had a revelation, I think. A young lady in my graduation class came into the cafeteria dancing, doing what we call whining, and the boys were all groveling. OK, first does this surprise anyone about men gawking. Then someone tells her a story. Lady D let's call her had a big booty and was raised very religiously. She stated out loud to a group of us that if a guy requested her to dance to the cafeteria line, she didn't mind doing it. Sexism much? The hardest thing to digest was hearing her say she was raised in a home that attended church four to five days a week. She stated she had a strict upbringing to us earlier that week in the ladies' dorms due to her religion. Lady D said she was out of her home; she was free to party and not to attend church anymore. Mental note to self: that doesn't sound good, right? Wait, I am nothing like lady D. This is the part of the story when you cover your ears. Am I doing the same thinking or acting in similar ways? Jesus and I are still associates, so I'm just taking an early adult sabbatical.

Sophomore year back at college after a long summer off. I'm back in New York earning some cash and single now that my boyfriend of almost four years and I broke up. Within the first week of returning to school, I got the Tea dished to me. Lady D got pregnant in the first year and dropped out of school. Whoa, kiss my cross! I may need to rejoin our school's Bible study club, and so I did. Jesus, I haven't forgotten about you. I've been just doing me. In fact, I'm going to need you to come through with the financial aid package. My parents refused to sell the S500. These are jokes. We never even owned a Mercedes. We didn't own A Lexus Coupe or a BMW. We just used our legs, caught taxis, buses, and frequent rides from family and friends. I thought then that God and I were back on track, so let's get back to those parties!

I had just recently become exposed to sororities and fraternities. I had the grades and decided I would like to join one or two potential sororities. While I narrowed down which one, I would simply observe until I decided. Watching some of these older girls was cool. What I most admired about them is that they were educated, had good grades, and were serving the public and the community.

Before doing this, I decided I would improve my GPA. I decided to be more social, so I increased my off-campus parties with friends and meeting the locals. I learned an unbelievably valuable lesson from this. Most of the local men who didn't attend college were also loco. Yikes! These men were simply taking advantage of young ignorant college women because they knew that they could. Many of them had no plans or obvious future for themselves. Most of these guys were not about anything significant, so I decided I would find myself a man in college.

Have you ever met someone that sparked your interest but it's out of your normal choice of options because they seem different? Well, sometimes this can be good and sometimes bad. Smiley was so different from other men I had encountered prior to him. He had a positive, fresh face and was engaging. I chose to have casual and intentional interactions with him, but nothing too serious. Just one year prior, I met CP, and I knew I shouldn't have entertained him, but everything is for a reason. (Isn't that biblical? I think it is.)

The condensed version is that with my new relationship, I had convenience. I dumped a high school boyfriend who was entertaining girls to choose the guy who would later become my daughter's father. Free cable and off-site dining were complimentary as well as being able to watch anime at his off-campus apartment. Did I tell you all I am an anime lover? Not yet, I didn't. We were OK for a time, but there were signs I ignored that we shouldn't be together. I tried early in this relationship to talk about God and asked if he believed in Jesus. I was never given a straight answer about this from my then boyfriend. He was Caribbean and his family may have learned other practices. What they were, I am not sure, but they were contrary to my beliefs and upbringing. Now that I am older and more learned in my faith, I am aware that some people entertain other things like familiar spirits and tarots to speak to them about people and circumstances. I don't believe or play with the devil!

After two years of dating this guy, I got the shock of my life that I wasn't planning for. I got pregnant in my senior year of college. Even after being pursued junior year by Smiley and turning him down. It was time to pull out and dust off the "good book" again and get back to Jesus. I was going to need him and all his help to get through this. Then

I got a second bomb dropped on me in the same year. I didn't have enough credits for my major that year to graduate. I was told I would need an extra year of classes and I was no longer able to live on campus being preggo. I was out of money and out of plans and knew this was when I had to tell my parents. I told my mother who was so disappointed in me, but she made me tell the news to my father and he was utterly devastated.

My father thought so highly of me. I think he had secretly lived vicariously through me, and he wanted me to go farther in education than he ever would. That I did do. He felt I gave up my dream for a man and because of this, he thought I was ruined. I would make it my life goal to show him I had created a life for myself that involved education and a career. He did get to see that I graduated college with my bachelor's degree, had a baby, and raised her. Dad never got a chance to see me in a career in healthcare. Today he rests in Heaven, but I promise you, Dad, with every breath I have left, I will continue to meet new goals and make greater accomplishments than these.

CHAPTER 3

DUMB, DEPRESSED, AND DUMPED

Move over Rahab. I was the whore of pre-med! I felt god-awful and hung my head in shame as I finished that fourth school year on campus. I was often talked about and laughed at, that I am sure of. I would abort my plans of going to med school to be a neurosurgeon and that was it for me. Then I had a dean tell me to come see him so he could share some info on how I could still possibly graduate. He created a plan that allowed me to do two summer sessions, then transfer to my home college in New York to finish my needed credits. It just required I continue to keep my grade point average up and that I get an approval from the head dean of my department. I was so grateful that this was approved so RIP Dean Archer, who recently passed last year. He told me that I was bright and could make it and that many young women like me had gotten caught up in the same situation. I was so humbled that someone so educated and inspirational could believe in me. This helped me to re-focus and finish my classes, then have my baby and graduate.

Just one thing remained. I would have to decide what to do about or say to Smiley! I decided for some time to avoid him. He knew I had a boyfriend and though we were like best friends calling each other at night, he wouldn't notice, right away. Then it happened: my belly grew big and was visible. I went out of my way to avoid him on campus because he was my friend and I cared about hurting him. Then one day the inevitable happened. I walked out of my dorm to class, and I ran into Smiley with a small group of his friends walking in the opposite direction. I held my breath, and I couldn't for long because I would choke this baby. My heart felt wild and was beating hard like it was in my throat. I said hello then he did a quick stare at my belly then disregarded me. Oh God, I just lost a good one!

I settled for what was familiar. If I could offer one piece of advice to anyone seeking love, it would be not to settle for anything. Expectations are not only fruitful, but are needed in life. Expect the best and set expectations in your relationships. Love yourself and family, but the greatest of all is to love God! I put a man first and before my needs and even God and because of this, I was crushed. I put man before myself and my knowledge and teachings of God, and I was a fool.

Now that you know I went through a season of depression, let's talk about how I was dumped. Dumped like we do the leftovers of our dinner plates into the garbage. Thrown away like an old, used pair of sneakers. Discarded like a leftover bottle of foundation after you know that little expiration date at the bottom was way since past. Yes, my worst fear came to life. The father of my new newborn daughter dumped me. What in the butter and biscuits was I going to do now? The first thing I knew was that my baby and I were headed home.

Here is where I would have the support to fall apart in the safety of my family. I was stripped bare and utterly heartbroken, having nothing left but a feeling of being raw. It's then that I knew exactly what was needed, and it was that I needed to get back to GOD. I humbled myself and went back, just like the prodigal daughter. I'm back living in a community that said I would never make it out. This made me feel like I was a failure. This couldn't be right, and I would never give in! Sundays led me back to the judgmental Baptist church that I grew up in and now I was a single mother. While many of these people turned up their noses and wrote me off, thank God that he did not. Today, I know that it wasn't church hurt; it was people hurt. I was so consumed with their opinions of me that I forgot none of them were perfect, either. In fact, no one on this Earth is perfect. Living back in Long Island meant I was back in my over-crowded family apartment. My new plan was to take the time to heal my broken spirit and then eventually move out and forward.

Here is a revelation that may help someone, and that is that God can use brokenness to make us over. I use this time back in New York to renew my relationship in my faith and with God. When I left home at eighteen for college, I was over going to church and with my faith. Wrong! I've learned that God is a creator and an architect. He can get us to our simplest composition, then rebuild and regenerate us outside. Over the next three years I immersed myself in my faith and in church. I regularly attended church with my daughter several times a week. I participated in Bible schools and in concerts. I was also reading and studying my Bible like never before.

One thing I forgot is that I needed to mention something to you. For a brief time, but on two separate occasions, I moved in with the daughter of my father. Young ladies, please let me offer you some advice. If a boyfriend offers to move you into a home and there is no commitment, then don't do it! There is an old cliché that says, "Why buy the cow when you can get the milk for free?" A free W.A.P. is a used W.A.P. and since we are keeping this Christian, this acronym means Woman Answering Prayers. (That is what you all were thinking, right?) The answer to that is he won't. Don't move in with a man you're not married to in my opinion. I came quickly to my senses that being with someone for convenience or because it was familiar is different from being in love.

About two months into living together, I became very lonely and was often left alone in his family house getting to know people I'd just met and who may not have favored me even being there. (God, what did I get myself into?) I lived in the basement with my child and father of the baby and was invited up for dinner. My mom would call me from time to time to check in on me and baby girl. I was twenty-two and an adult, so she couldn't force me to move back home because, as I told her, I was grown. This doesn't mean she agreed with my choice of living in this way. She would rather me live at home in a crowded apartment with the love of my family than to live in a basement like an adopted little redhead child. My mom made my day when one day she told me she had heard from Smiley, Yup, I said it. She says he was calling her home more frequently and asking how I was doing and if she had heard from me. He would ask her how me and my new baby were doing.

I decided to stand up for myself and make an ultimatum and that began the unraveling. Young people, be incredibly careful out there. Such a thing exists called a soul tie. It is easy to get caught and tangled in, but to unravel is a challenging thing. I would ask my daughter's father when he was going to propose and when we would marry. I shared with him that my life plan included being married and having a family and being some man's wife. We looked at circulars of jewelry shops and before leaving me for a five-day trip, he said we would discuss this when he returned. I waited anxiously and had even circled two potential rings that I thought I would love. CP came back home two weeks later, and he didn't want to discuss the rings or marriage. He hits me with a stunner, saying I should take the baby and move home with my mom. I was told a fallacy about how he was moving back to VA and getting an apartment and that he'd send for us later to join him. In the meantime, he suggested I enroll in the local community college and finish the credits I needed to graduate with my college degree.

Now that I caught you up to speed, let's move forward. After a few months of being separated from my boyfriend, he called me and told me the relationship was over. He suggested the baby and I could still move back in with him, but it would be for a co-parenting type of situation. I was back on Long Island living with my family at the time. That day I decided to put off all men. No, I didn't like women but would take an oath of celibacy, and it worked for a time. I had an intermittent date every quarter or so. The local New York men never had the thing I was searching for, so dating would only be casual. I wanted to love someone and for them to love me back. Since I couldn't find what I was looking for, I simply stopped looking. I could give all my love to God. Then what would I do next? I would kiss my cross. My revelation was then of the depth Christ had first loved me. When men left me, I had to learn Jesus never would. My eyes were then open, and my heart quickened. In layman's terms, my lashes were batting, and my heart was "beating out of my chest."

I learned a great deal in this period of my life. Over the next three to four years, I would become one of the world's best parents, single or not! I would be a better child to my parents and even be a better person to my siblings. The most important thing though that happened to me was that I would become a stronger Christian. I learned in this that If I stray, God can always draw me back. I could fall and still climb the ranks again to be elevated in my faith walk because God still loves me. It was at this time I would apply a Biblical lesson to the Biblical scripture to ask, and I shall receive. I got it. I would ask God for a husband. Lord, now that we are cool, please send me a husband and a father to my kid.

Just then I decided to date again. Ex boyfriends wouldn't work because they were stuck in the past, but I grew. Some of the newly met guys were snakes and I could weed them out like a gardener. Then it came to me, and I got another revelation. I was twenty-three years old and now a college graduate who loved God and had lots of free energy. My body I had read was to be the temple of the living God. Well, this temple was about to be a brickhouse! I took myself to the local gym and began to exercise up to five days weekly. I would run two to three miles daily, then play hand ball daily as well. I would work out one to two hours on weights in the local recreation center, then do one hour of aerobics at night at home.

Sitting in church one Sunday, I had an epiphany. There, I told God specifically what I wanted in a man. Okay, then I would have to think things through. Dear God, hear my prayer:

God, give me a husband:

Who does not have more than one child.

Who is a dark-skinned and tall Black man.

Who is college educated and well versed.

Who has a good credit score and a bank account.

Now I may not remember today everything I included on this list. I can tell you I wrote this list on a piece of paper, and I would often pull it out and edit it. I changed the prayer to asking God to give me a man with no children, who comes from a good family. A man who knows God and who would accept and love my child as his own. Trust me, I knew then that God would listen to specifics. As I searched New York for the list, I was coming up with zero hits. I kept my eyes on God. I was told to seek God and his kingdom and everything else would be added to me. Then, would you believe it? Smiley called my mother's house to check in on me, and what he didn't know was that I had moved back home.

Divine plans and timing are a real thing. My buddy was genuine over the phone and caring, and it felt so good to be able to connect with him again. It had been so long since we had spoken. My heart grew just a little bit bigger than the meanie in that Christmas movie, hah! We talked on the phone that day for hours. Smiley became my long-distance telephone friend. He lived twenty-two hours or in flight time, two hours away, but we had a great phone relationship. Stop. I know that you 've heard long-distance relationships don't work, but they can if the bond is right.

I never had a phone relationship with anyone in which we talk for hours over the phone. However, talking with him seemed so easy. I am not even sure he is interested in me or my baby. God, I don't know how I am supposed to do this. I wasn't. I just needed to be myself and naturally allow the plan that was unfolding for my life to take place. My mother's side of the family was from Florida. I informed my homey that I was planning to attend our family reunion this year with my then three-year-old daughter. To my surprise, Smiley blew my mind! He decided he would drive the three hours to meet my family and daughter, Oh Lord! This was all so new.

Then, I not just got a call from Smiley, but he also asked me for my hotel address. My family is running rampant throughout the hotel, and I am about to get the shock of my life. I would have formed the cross symbol with my hand, but I wasn't Catholic, so I may have gotten the directions wrong. Forgive me. Just like that, there he is. Voila. Now at my first look at my friend who I missed and hadn't seen in years, I noticed something. I had the image all wrong. That smile was full of mischief, and I knew what he reminded me of.

I knew my college friend Smiley was from Florida, but I didn't expect he would come to one of my family reunions. He had never even met my family. First, let's use this term reunion loosely. My family had a fish fry planned, a pool day outing, a trip to Disney for those who could afford it, and a day to attend a church where the pastor was a distant cousin. Might I say he was a sexist and thought women should be quiet and didn't belong preaching in the church. I wonder what he would think twenty-plus years later today of all the ladies who preach and speak for themselves.

My mom did me a favor that weekend. She extended an invitation for Smiley to stay with us. I didn't have a lot of money at that time. I would work little retail jobs until I got my dream job of working in a hospital. My dad didn't accompany us to the reunion, so my mom and I in my room rented double queen beds. Mom took my daughter to the bed with her and allowed me and Smiley to lay together in the bed. We were told don't do any funny business, but you know. Who was looking if we were quiet? (He He) I wished my preacher cousin was there to see that! The reunion itself was good, I guess. No. I am not throwing shade, but that cousin still irks me. My mom told me not to say anything to him being he was older than her, but I promise you neither my daughter, Smiley, nor I attended his church.

Friends from college life became sparse and previous friends from high school seemed to handle me differently after I graduated from college. I didn't have a lot of money then so I couldn't afford to get a separate room after paying for plane tickets. It was a good thing for me that Mom didn't argue with me on this. In many ways, she allowed me to have an opportunity that would lead me into my future. Smiley had obligations back at his home down south, so he could only stay overnight one night and a half day the next morning.

On the bright side of this, my three-year-old was enjoying her first trip to sunny Florida. She would pop her bubblegum in her mouth in her colorful short set. Baby girl was cute and sassy, looking like a little chocolate "Powerpuff Girl." The next day, after waking up, we took a trip to the local mall like a little blended family. My daughter fell in love with a giant, life-sized, stuffed Dora the Explorer doll and I immediately tell her no because this plush thing was over forty dollars. We walk out of the store and as we proceed to walk away Smiley comes out and hands her the doll he purchased, and I scowl. From that moment, I realized how committed my friend was to being in good graces with my daughter and making me happy.

What an epiphany! This guy that was the friendliest and most kind to me was a gem. He was a true diamond, and I was like a smiling little kid. Did I say that I am an artist or that I am eclectic and that I love most things fantasy including books? I don't know why God gave me such a brain, but I love color, fashion, and imagination. My Chessy was so full of mystery and intrigue with a mischievous smile that created a small buzz in my heart. What I didn't tell you is that I didn't think he was my type. Now I realize that the young heart hardly knows what it likes but picks people based on physical attraction, mostly. My ideal guy had to be masculine and socially thriving, have a sense of personal style, and, Lord, let him be a good sexual partner.

Now listen to me, Linda. Today I know that there are more important things to look for in a partner. Then I was a twenty-year-old rebel and HBCU graduate and a mom. Parents, this doesn't mean to unenroll your kids from an HBCU or college. We were all once at this stage or are there now, so give people grace. Trust that the discipline you taught them in their upbringing and giving them a sense of self-respect will be enough to sustain them. For the things you cannot see, pray and drink a glass of wine or the beverage of your choice.

CHAPTER 4

WHINE, WEAVES, AND WAIT A MINUTE

If you have ever had a "dirty whine dance" then you have surely had them all. For those who are not familiar, come close and I will explain this word. "Whining" refers to a provocative dance that generated from Jamaican dancehall music. It involves dancing closely with someone while grinding and gyrating your genitals together and often to dancehall music. In college this was a way for me to celebrate how hard I studied and worked during the week. I would spend my weekend nights dolling up my hair and putting on a fresh new outfit and getting to the parties from Friday through Saturday and sometimes Sundays. (Lord help me.)

Jesus, maybe I shouldn't be praying this, but I am talking to you right? Lord, please give me the ability to be hot and courageous. I have short hair and always have but grew up with two older sisters. The two of them taught me how to put in hair extensions and hair weaves like it was nobody's business. They would make me sew in their tracks for parties and dances then leave me on my own to figure out doing my own hair. Thankfully, I met a group of female friends, and we would take turns practicing doing our own hair. This helped teach me how to do my own hair and gain independence from not having to wait on someone else to make myself look good.

On club nights I would take the time to apply a fresh hair weave. I would spend the day hours going to the mall after class and buying a new outfit. Next, I would sit down in front of my mirror and spend the time applying make-up. At that time, it would consist of lipstick and kohl black eye liner. I know ladies, today this would not be considered a "full on beat." The next most important thing was the pre-party dance. This was always maximized by consuming a little liquid courage. I am by nature an introverted extrovert. (Make it make sense, Jesus.) I don't know how to fully explain this, but I guess it would be said that as an introvert partying, alcohol turns me into another person. I become wilder and more adventurous. Let me say here that alcohol isn't good for us. Furthermore, cheap alcohol like that owned by college students will do you in. Adults say to do all things in moderation but when it comes to drinking it's best if you just don't do it.

What I will say is that consuming it made me a little more outspoken. I was more comfortable dancing with guys and more sexually prone. In hindsight I realized that this isn't such a good thing and the problem I had was a self-esteem issue. My self-esteem issues developed from my childhood. As we grow older and with some help we can get healing from these issues. To grow we need to heal from our past and then turn around and help someone else who is coming behind us. In the future I plan to do this by starting a 501c3 organization for teen girls that helps with developing future skills, teaching finance, and combating low self-esteem.

My household was composed of women. Women in my family dominated. Originally, there was six of us and it had not always been that way. My mom and grandmother raised four children. My dad at that time was divorced from his previous marriage after which he moved in with us later. Now before you come for me, I will willingly lay things bare. I came from a dysfunctional blended family, and I am learning that a lot of people do.

We grew up in poverty and lived in low-income housing. Even though this was the case we were still a little better off because my dad had two jobs. I was exposed to a lifestyle that was a little bit better than being low income because of dad and his provision. We may not have had a lot of money at that time, but we had a lot of love. Our mom didn't know how to do hair even having three daughters so thank God for our grandmother. Back then our hair was neat and clean then pressed straight but it wasn't very stylish. Our grandmother would use pressing combs and Blue Nile hair grease to straighten our hair via stove top. (Pft, if she thinks she is getting me in the chair with that hot comb she has another thing coming.) Then I would do the most logical thing. Duck and run and get cussed out but Jesus knew my heart. LOL! Eventually, I did lose, though. Then I would sit down in a seat and get my hair pressed straight with a hot comb. Next she would part our hair into square sections then twist our hair and apply barrettes at the end. Here is a caveat, this is how we styled Black hair in the late eighties, as flat irons didn't exist then. My biggest issue was I was called a Tom Boy then so I would always mess up my hair before the end of the day. I would lose the bows, ribbons, and barrettes and my hair would unravel and be wild by days end. This would make the boys tease me and call me ugly, but who cared? I was having the time of my life growing up. Now that I am older and know better, many of the boys were ugly, too. Let me have this one, please. Trust me, I know today we don't respond like that. In fact, many people who are not great looking in your youth may turn out to look much better as adults.

I warned you that I was a rough little girl, yes? I climbed fences and tore and ripped clothes and shoes on a regular basis. I was a chocolate girl with a beautiful smile, a big nose, and acne. As I grew older, I was able to get the acne under control, but the nose was here to stay. Today I know that lots of African American people have wide noses, and I did grow into mine. Lastly, I was the third daughter in the family, so I had to inherit my two older sisters' clothing. This today is one of the reasons I am so into having my own fashion and sense of style. When you grow up poor and your family is trying to survive, you often must do whatever is required of you to fit the best interests of the family.

Me with my kinky hair, active child behavior, acne, and wide nose wearing used clothing left me with low self-esteem. I was smart and quiet until you got to know me. I was bullied so often that you did nothing until you felt backed into a corner. Once you took me there, though, I would box you like Tyson! My older siblings were seven and eight years older than me and my younger brother was five years younger than me. I went to school by myself and after being bullied for so long I decided to fight back. So fighting was my defense mechanism. It was easy, and I wouldn't hesitate to do it. You would be shocked when people encountered a quiet girl like me who would fight like the last episode of an anime showdown cartoon. Jesus made and knew me so then He knows that I am a fighter. The bullies embarrassed me then tested me, but they did "catch these hands." For the next five years I would keep the bullies away, boost my self-esteem, and kick ash! (I know you thought your girl was going to slip up and cuss there.) Then I heard a voice in my head. Something told me this wasn't the way to get attention or boost esteem. Now I wish that I hadn't heard this, but I know I was convicted.

God puts something special inside each of us. We are all given an assignment, and it is the reason we exist on Earth. We live out a set of experiences and develop certain skill sets that can be used by God. Everything we have been through can be used by God to get glory out of our lives. I may have had low self-esteem and had to wear used clothing, but God gifted me with resilience. I am a natural born fighter who loves laughter and comedy. I have been a single mother and am a first-time college graduate in my family. My love is for anime, fashion, comedy, and loving God I will use all of these avenues to move my future forward in this life. Fighters like me are known for fighting with everything we have. Since I matured, I have learned I no longer need to fight the way I used to. I now have God fight my battles because he fights spiritually. If he is fighting for me, I don't need to. Just don't test me because it is still in me. I do love fantasy and the arts and most of all to live in the light of God.

At eight years old I discovered that I could draw. In school I would create posters that would be displayed in my local city library. In church I was a member of the youth and young adult choirs. I would often get assigned to sing a song but because of my vocal range being between alto and tenor, I would shy away from performing but always look forward in secret to singing until I blew someone's socks off! Early in my youth I discovered the love of dancing and was a natural at it. In school I would enter competitions to perform dancing and became well known because of it. Be it art, song, or dance, God would use it all to shape my future. My question then was how does God plan to use these skills that I have acquired through the years? He can use my art to display his love for the people in this world, use my sense of laughter, comedy, and dance to bring joy. He can use my hands to help those with healing and to apply however he fits. Most of all he could use the battles I have come through with my health to encourage people that he can heal. My journey on the path of the cross started in my youth.

At eleven years old I walked down the middle aisle of my church to the alter to receive Christ. Truth be told I wasn't sure what all that entailed. It could have been like I was receiving a free pack of stickers or something. My pastor of that time was elegant and sophisticated and was articulate. I knew that when he was issuing the call to Christ that something (Holy Spirit) was telling me to come, that I needed to. I also felt that if having Jesus could make me as posh and smart as he was, I was all in, sign me up!

Leading up to accepting the call was a process. I would attend church often and every week and it felt like every sermon preached was being directed towards me. It had been what felt like weeks or months of being prompted to go up when I finally got the courage one Sunday. Scared and shaking I accepted JESUS (no stickers included) and it felt great. So that was that, and I was told that based on my confession I was now saved. (Hold it!) The minister went on to say that as a demonstration of faith I would need to be baptized in water. Does this man know that I can't swim, Jesus? Now that I said yes to Jesus does this mean like he is taking me here and now? Not on my watch he isn't.

At home over the week, I talked to my older sisters since they had been through this already. My older sister encouraged me to say it will be easy and the other sister warns me I am going to drown. (She was just messing with me, people.) My middle sister got a kick out of teasing me. Well, that makes my choice super easy. I decide then to say no to baptism. Turns out that even though I said no my parents said yes. The next Sunday I conceded to being baptized. Purposely, I wore the wrong color, and it didn't matter as everyone was given an all-white robe to wear. A group of teens and myself were all taken downstairs in the church to be prayed over before going in the water. For me this was good because deep water and I were not friends. When it was my turn, I was escorted upstairs and into a small, heated backroom that held a small, four-foot-deep wading pool. In it were four adults including the minister. It was now or never!

I looked around and noticed there was an echo of old hymns, moaning, and praying being sung until the minister stood before me. I was extremely nervous before even entering the water. Next thing I was led down into the pool and the pastor came to stand at a position near or above my head behind me. Suddenly he placed his hand over my forehead and after praying dunked me into the water and kept me down there for what I felt was about one minute. I began to panic and grabbed onto the closest solid thing in reach, which was the sleeve of his robe. That day both the pastor and I were being baptized whether he liked it or not! To this day I swear he may have shaken me from side to side a little bit down under the water to free up the sin off of me! When I came out of the water, it was different. I felt several emotions being relieved, feeling confused and cold. Of all these, mostly I remember the cold which reminded me of a refreshing sensation which I will never forget. The water or pool wasn't different, I was. This was finally over and now I could move forward. Seven years later, I entered college, and I would take Jesus and all that I had learned through my Christian faith and upbringing and put them in a pocket for a later time.

At eighteen, I decided it was time to part ways with my religion for a time. I had a boyfriend of two years and was graduating high school. I was on my way to a new beginning and that meant I would start in a new state of mind. My relationship with my siblings was changing in so many ways. My sisters were both in their late twenties and were living their own lives. My brother was thirteen and at home with Mom and Dad. My choice for college was over an eight-hour drive away. I would take the Bible and Lord knows I ended up needing it. During my adolescence the Bible was difficult to read and follow. Today we can use different versions that help us to understand more clearly. When I was homesick or lonely or depressed, I would open my Bible and read it. To help make it more exciting, I would use multicolored highlighters to bookmark certain words.

By reading the Bible every so often I was learning in small increments about God. Yes, I was baptized and knew that he accompanied me everywhere, though I hadn't yet developed a deep relationship with God. Yes, I went to a Historically Black College and University or HBCU. We would argue about people stealing your paid dryer when you took too long to recover your clothes. The weekends were made of loud rap music, dating, and hanging out with the locals. God is and has been good to me even when I was not good. He loves wild people and even nerdy introverted extroverts like me. What I did learn is that he died to try and redeem us all and that includes all spectrums of people, all people.

God has more forgiveness and gives us more mercy than any of us deserve. He is our creator and yet demonstrates how we should model him when we deal with other people.

Better Him than me. I am grateful God didn't leave me in control of other people. He knew that if he had. likely, I would smite them all like *Bruce Almighty*. No, wait, in the words of the late, great Maya Angelou, "When we know better, we do better." It took until my adult life to realize that when situations presented themselves, I should and must take the "higher way up." Say, what? That's right, I was this-years-old when I learned that when it comes to people being out of order and missing the mark, it includes myself.

So here we are at the part of the book where I must do some self-reflection. In past times and current I have been a twerp. Not ruined all the time or condescending that I think. I have often been extremely sarcastic and not always considerate of my words. I learned from my youth that if I was being bullied and couldn't defend myself to always retaliate with a snappy comeback verbally. That is until I learned to stand and fight. Doing this kept people feeling bad about engaging to attack or intimidate me. Now in the world we live in today schools deal more seriously with bullying. When I was a kid, you would learn to deal with being picked on and keep moving forward. Today I recognize that in my past my love language was sarcasm, and it was a guard.

I've done some self-reflection and now have changed. The only shield that I need is God. Today my love language is giving something to someone that will give them joy. I know one thing: growth is a mother-sucker. Growing pain is a real thing even internally, spiritually. One of the hardest things to do is to surrender our will. With me, being a strong personality type who is by nature relentless, it is crushing. It's so hard to give up control and in all honesty, I hate it and do not want to. This is just what the Master wants from us. He doesn't want to break our wills but wants us to surrender our plans to His.

One of the best ways to overcome this is having to give willingly to others and be generous. Putting my needs after someone else at times helps me to build patience. It also is a gift of the Holy Spirit. Well, hello H.S. Did you forget someone? No. Having patience slows me down. It causes me to listen to God and trust him for answers. Then we could propose always multitasking is of the devil, hah! When we get quiet and be still, we can hear from God. By slowing down we can do things more precisely, giving it more time and attention so it can become exceptional. This is why we should apply patience often and where needed.

CHAPTER 5

SPIRIT FRUIT

Now today there is a spiritual trait I am currently working on developing called gentleness. Growing up being a physical, rough girl I was an active child. I was a wild card taking unnecessary risks and not afraid to get into a good fist fight. I began to learn and understand around the age of eighteen that this wasn't quite ladylike. Then what was a lady supposed to be like? My grandma, my mother, and two sisters were all women, but did that make them ladies? I soon discovered that a lady was dainty. She was gentle, beautiful, soft, and poised. Well, then, that's it. I decided I would be a lady. Where did I sign up? I would become a lady if it was the last thing I did. First, I had to buy shoes and ladies were elegant. Well, I'm going to need a job then. Until I got the dream job in my college education field I would work in retail. I spent the next few years building myself up to become more ladylike. I knew if I became more feminine, softer, and sweeter, I could be a lady in no time.

Back then, I didn't earn a lot of money so I would resort to sketching the clothes I could see myself wearing one day. I had to challenge some of the customs I was brought up with. My mother was a Christian but, in her anger, she would cuss you out. I don't believe a lady should resort to doing this. She should whisper a soft rebuke to you to sway your opinion. Today I have kids and as a mom I now understand at times they make you want to cuss them out but, exhale. OK so now that we have an idea what the behavior should be like of a lady let's move on to looks. I knew that most ladies were beautiful and charismatic, and beauty required makeup.

As a teen I hated to wear full-face glam makeup unlike the young ladies of today. I was told that makeup was for hussies. Certain colors of lipstick and nail polish were not allowed to be worn in our house. My grandmother told us these colors were for whores only. Well, Grandma, I have news for you, you are wrong. Hoes could wear every color of lipstick and nail polish and even no makeup! My grandma is gone now. She is resting with Christ, so I can tell her this. I can say before she left the earth at eighty-three, she even reconsidered and started to wear colored nail polish. She was wrong about that, and I was right, so there! Fix it, Jesus, why are we like this?

Back to makeup… my makeup of choice was kohl jet-black eyeliner and whatever shade of lipstick I could find. These were the final additions to my perfect look and gentle feminine hello. Less was more and still today I am somewhat like this when applying makeup. My makeup of the year of 2000 was in that day what I would call beat at least I thought. Now let's go down the lady checklist together. I was becoming more patient and gentler and less masculine, less hood. Then my dad taught me a lesson I would never forget. He told me as a woman and as a person overall the phrase you can catch more bees with honey. His lesson was golden and to this day I still applied his rule. When you deal with people in life, it is just nice to be kind and you get more help from people and genuine care when you are this way.

Well, Dad, I am not a beekeeper. At one time in my life kindness was not my thing. I'd rather suck my teeth and roll my eyes and spit fire at anyone who tried to test me. Behaving this way I would have to ask myself WWJD? Well Jesus is much nicer than I have ever been but I'm getting better. Jesus would want me to be kind to people even when they don't deserve it. Why? Because he's kind to me when I don't deserve it. This is a challenging thing for sure to do. Hello, my name is Lynette. Although I haven't perfected it, I am currently practicing being kind. Sounds stupid, right? Moving forward, I'll find out that being like God means we carry the fruits of the Holy Spirit.

Ok, this sounds good to me and who doesn't love fruit? Well, this isn't the edible fruit that you digest. These fruits are attributes of the Holy Spirit. You received the Holy Spirit as a gift from when you confess God and Jesus as your Lord. He then comes into your heart and lives with you for the eternity of your life. Some of the traits of having him are love, peace, patience, kindness, faithfulness, gentleness, and self-control. Having a basket of these fruits would create within you a better person all over.

I wasn't just becoming a lady. At this point, I was becoming a Christian. Now for me some of this came easy, and some did not. I was thinking I had a good handle on practicing these values except for a few. I've been tethering too long with faithfulness. I'm getting better but not perfect at this. My work in progress fruit seems to be self-control. Daily, weekly, and often I wrestle to be led by controlling myself. I tend to indulge too much in several things. Too much access has been given to my flesh in eating, drinking, and intimacy. I love food, wine, and sex. I must put limits on my flesh, so my spirit stays in control. Today what helps me with this is praying, staying close to God daily. Listening to old sermons, attending weekly Bible studies, and reading my Bible or fasting helps me. On this Earth we're not perfect but we should strive to live holy and try to be the best version of ourselves always.

I am a thick Black woman who was teased earlier in school for this, but I know today that many people enjoy this type of look and physique. I like to consider myself a foodie. This is someone who loves to try and experience different cuisines of food. We like to use this word nowadays, don't we? Realistically, though, we must eat to live and not live to eat. As humans we love to indulge and sometimes overindulge in pleasure. Self-control is one of the most challenging traits to demonstrate and maintain.

Now let's move forward to alcohol. First, I must acknowledge that my father growing up was a beer drinker. I grew up watching my dad drink six packs of his favorite Budweiser beers, at least two or three cans at a time. That is until one day he quit and went cold turkey drinking and smoking cigarettes. I commend him for this. Although he is no longer here with us, he made a change to make his life better. In high school I was introduced to beer by local friends, and I didn't like the taste. My older sister, at this time being an adult already, would let me sip from her drinks. Occasionally, she would let me have a wine cooler or sip a mixed drink she would have or some wine. Later attending an HBCU I was given and offered more choices of drinks than most college students are.

Certain strong drinks I learned were not for me, but I learned to like fruity drinks or often coffee-like mixed drinks. After graduating college and becoming an adult I was introduced to different varieties of wine which I took a keen interest in. "It was the best of times, it was the worst of times," (lol) so my sister liked Zin which was not my friend. By the way, I forgot to tell you all I used to rap in my high school days. Anyway she wanted to give me a white wine, which was tart, but you could get a little buzz. Then I experimented with different wines until I found what I liked. I discovered that I like red wines the best. Today I also know that I like a variety of different wines but from certain grapes. In the wine world people have different acquired tastes and I was not the exception.

What I did know, from being a science major in college, was that alcohol wasn't good for the body. All things must be in moderation. Over the years of living and friendships I discovered that alcohol consumption allowed me to let my guard down some. My introvert was really introverting hard. Letting down our guard isn't always a good thing. Guards are much like fences in that they are meant to put a barrier around us. Walking in this Christian life requires you to be sober and of sound mind.

Recently, in 2017 and as a full-grown adult, I was gifted a wine fridge by my hubby. Some things I have learned since my childhood that have helped me: Kidney failure is a real disease and effects African Americans five times more than other races. In the year 2006 on my honeymoon cruise, I discovered tequila. We are not friends but are like frenemies. Tequila will make you happy today and repent tomorrow! Today I am in control, and I choose to avoid alcohol mostly and drink only on special occasions. Those occasions are holidays like the end of the year or birthdays or a family vacation. There are at times on weekends after working in healthcare, I celebrate the weekend by having a glass or two of red wine.

Moving on to control and how this affects intimacy and relations and its importance. In my youth I didn't know how to honor my temple as I should. The Bible talks about your temple being your body. It should be holy and acceptable unto God. This includes how you keep your temple, how you treat your temple, and how you care for your temple. I realized later by even getting tattoos it was dishonoring to my body, so I stopped after getting just three and a tongue piercing which I removed early. I realized that there may be children or teens reading this book so let's keep it simple. Intimacy doesn't equal just sex. I believe I spent years of life chasing this feeling. Later I discovered what I really needed was to feel covered and sheltered.

I found intimacy with God. To get there, though, he first had to break me. What I meant is that relationships had to fall off that I initiated or pursued of my own will. Once I was lonely and broken and submitted, he met me. After feeling down I stopped focusing on the act of sex and went in search of God. For three years I was focused, consumed, and engrossed with reading my Bible, attending church, praying, and worshipping. Then God turned around, and he blessed me. Yes, you heard me right and give me a minute to explain.

Prayer does really change things. Hallelujah! I was in great physical shape at this time, and I mean like a brick house. I was running weekly, lifting weights, and was abstinent. I could put in a hair weave and style my hair in under one hour. No one in my community could style clothes like me and my makeup was spot on. It was then at the time when I was not looking but suddenly received a marriage proposal. If you guessed that this was from my favorite male friend in college then you are right.

Well, look at Jesus. He sent me my life partner and who knew it would be someone I met earlier in life? To be truthful, I didn't think it would be someone from the past. I always figured it would be someone in the future I had not met. Immediately, I thought it was too late for someone to love me after having had a baby out of wedlock by someone else. I was so overjoyed that this man was willing to love me still. It reminded me of how God never gives up on us and how He still loved me. Even if we miss a door God can lay a path for us to get to the plan he has for us. God is the expert architect, and he creates and modifies a plan for our life. I am so very thankful he hasn't left me to live out this life all on my own. I love me and trust that I know myself, but I am not reliable alone. I am human and an introvert. I will go home and put on pajamas, read fantasy books, sip red wine, and watch K (Korean) dramas. Then get down and kneel the next day and pray for forgiveness because I am also not an idiot.

Now to address the elephant in the room. I had to reign in my love for sex. The lust of the flesh I have learned is a trick from Satan. Sex itself is a natural thing that God created for procreation and marital intimacy. While it is an act so is one of the chapters of the Bible. (I bet you didn't see that one coming?) What I love about sex is the natural endorphins you feel afterwards. The act itself is ok and there are different strategies and positions to get the deed done. The best sex happens and blooms in stages but is done best when there is a mental connection. You can have great sex when you are in lust with someone but have no other connection. You can feel like you had an out-of-body experience from sex. The sensation is even more hype when two people are in love.

Sex between a marital couple elevates things. It makes you strive higher and fight harder. Love makes you consider the other person and prioritize them even over yourself. It is light and strength with the ability to encompass all. Come take a love walk with me. I found love at the early age of sixteen (not really but it was puppy love). This was when I found my first boyfriend. We had about four to five months of dating until my father threatened him with violence. He was two years older than me and from the rough area of Brooklyn, New York. This wasn't a true love story, and it suddenly left me as quickly as it came. I was sad and depressed, and it took me some time before I let someone else in. At seventeen I took a second spin at love. A high school guy one class year younger than me took an interest in me. We decided to date, and, in this relationship, we spent a lot of time just hanging out as kids. This was a wonderful experience for me in that it modeled a lot of what true love should be like, but it was immature. In my heart I had renewed faith that this was love. Love for me meant spending a lot of time with someone. Well, yes and no to answer this. When you love someone, spending time with them is a carefree thing. In fact, time goes fast when you're making memories with the ones you love. I also know that you can love someone and be miles away. Some examples are long-distance love relationships. Another example is how we can love someone who has left the world already and transitioned. Love can cross all times and into eternity love is vast and never dies out.

Getting back to this junior love attempt makes me say that love is suffocating. It really isn't but when one person is in it more than the other it can seem haphazard. Then I thought maybe if I left for college, I could get some space from this dude. I wasn't mature enough at eighteen to tell him that perhaps we should take some time apart, so we could learn what we wanted ourselves individually from life. When you love someone, it is also necessary to have some distance between the two of you. I applied for local colleges in NY but accepted an offer for college in Virginia, knowing that would give me some distance from a three-year long relationship where we spent little time apart. This would give me almost one year to spend some time separately but still together because we did date long distance for a year. That was a creepy thing to do, Lynette. (Yup.)

You can smell that though, right? It smells like freedom. I got one solid year free from my young love other than phone conversations. It was then liberating until the unimaginable happened. He applied for a college twenty minutes from my own college in Virginia. (Sweet Jesus.) Well, love endures all, right? My second year of college I decided that I would be liberated. "Who the son set free was free indeed," says the Bible. I would gather up enough courage to tell him then the stars aligned. It was Christmas break and at this time of year college students sometimes go home with friends and not to their own homes. My boyfriend called me and told me that he had already started his Christmas break and was at home. Then he pulled my wig off! Ok, not literally, but he told me he brought a friend home to stay for winter break with them. The thing is she was a female, and his mom had given the OK for her to stay with them for five days. How could that have happened when for four years I was never even allowed to spend the night with him? Freak that! I decided at that moment to call it quits. Everyone I grew up with thought he and I would one day be married but no. I wish him well in life!

Listen up to all my young people out there. I need the attention of everyone under thirty who is single and not married. It is ok to love and to lose. You can love again and if it is not right the first time give yourself grace to love and be loved again. I can tell you I endured several young relationships before I found the love of my life. Be encouraged friends, it takes a little motion to get things right and timing is everything.

Here is another saying and that is the third times the charm, right? (Nope, not necessarily, but keep listening.) I took some time in between boyfriends and relations to enjoy and live my best life. My best living at that time was featured by the capital letter O. O as in options, opportunities, and best of all outstanding orgasms. We are all human and I am open about human anatomy and how our bodies function. I do have kids now so they may read this book. Therefore, I may have to soften the blow and say (mind y'all business) so next I must urge you to listen to that little voice inside of you. (I have not always.) I sat down in my third year of classes in college and met someone unintentionally. Being your girl, I want to save you from unnecessary future hurt and turmoil because I didn't see myself. Listen in closely so you save yourself from undue stress in your future. In the past I had a love for what I call "save someone else syndrome."

A guy I will call JC tried to aggravate me into liking him until one day he ran me down. He'd frustrate me by asking for college supplies or ask for answers to homework because he knew I was smart. He would have no other way to talk to me without small talk. I had a boyfriend in the past, but this was different. This guy played me into liking him. Not because he was unattractive or not charming but because he was the opposite of everything I was. Sometimes we may think opposites are good and at times it is but for me this became very bad. He explained his dyslexia and asked for my extra help with classwork and homework and my dumb self took the bait. Word to the wise is that although you can be kind to all people don't be taken advantage of. You should not lower your standards to personally feel you must rescue everyone. You can point them to a resource that can help them, like I should have.

I entered this relationship, and it lasted for four years. I provided tutoring for free and companionship and in turn received the use of an off-campus apartment and a sexual relationship without commitment. I take ownership that I played a part of this relationship of my own free will. This is why I say God don't leave me alone to make choices by myself. With this I would like to say that I did not get hugged enough as a child. Parents hug your children, tell them how special they are, and that you love them. Children, youth, it is ok to receive love. Honest love not based on manipulation is safe. When we don't give this love to our children, they spend a lifetime looking for it in someone else. God is love. We spend our lives here in pursuit of finding this kind of love. Now that I have addressed the youth it is time to share with the adults.

CHAPTER 6

TIME FOR THE D

Let's start this chapter by addressing the elephant in the room. Sis, break out your good wine and post up your emojis. The D is a term of endearment for the male reproductive organ. First let me say that I am a feminist at heart. Next, I'd like to say that adults have a need to experience physical connection and if possible, a love that satisfies. The ladies may jump me when they see me, but we put too much emphasis on "the D"! In case you have yet to figure it out this is an abbreviation for, you guessed it, Dees Nuts (just kidding). Some call it ding-a Ling and others say dildo or it's also known as the shortened nickname for the name Richard.

Keep in mind, as I said before, children may be reading this, even mine because they are nosey. I put myself in the category with the other ladies above because I too am guilty of expecting mind blowing D. We should not resort to reducing people to the amount of pleasure they give us. Intimacy can and does take place in the mind first as a thought. This is why the Bible says as a man thinks so is he or she. Therefore, it is important to take your time and make meaningful connections with people. Having the right spouse or partner and mind frame can make love an out-of-body experience. Some even believe you can make love without physical contact. To my YA readers come back and find me once you become of legal age!

Now that the D is out of the bag lets address it properly. It is simply a piece of connective tissue. I know, don't break down on this part if you haven't already. Stay strong and remember we learned this back in health class. I just want us to see that we put too much emphasis on this. Now that we have killed the flesh let's dive into the real deal. The D we need to put into perspective that brings and keeps us closer to God is devotion.

Devotion is defined as to have love, loyalty, and enthusiasm for a person's activity or cause. Once that I learned I wanted to have a relationship with God it was important for me to prioritize devotion. Let's make this very simple to follow. Many of the stars today have their own camps of supporters which are avidly and generally devoted. Some examples of this are our favorite musicians, actors, and even sports teams. Football fans have their teams, chicken lovers have Popeyes and Chick-fil-A, Amazon has prime members. Christians, we need an unyielding, never relenting faith and devotion in God and Jesus.

Let's dive into this topic and dispel some hearsay. First, I want to say that no sin is too big that God can't forgive. Evil wants us to believe that we have done too much to get back in good standing with the creator. This is a lie. Even the Bible talks about before we were formed in our mama's womb that God knew us. This tells me that before God created us, he knew what we would be like and what choices we were making in life. Man, the best part about this is despite our bad choices in sin or contrary lifestyle the father is still waiting for us to choose Him. Yes, I know I told Him, and some people will not like this statement saying, "Why do you tell Him?" I can share that I got into an argument with a coworker a few years ago about this. She argued me down and told me that God could be a woman. Earlier, I told you all I like to fight, so I argued back.

My argument was that the Bible stated God our *father*. Today, I still stand firm on his belief. However, as I grow, I have learned how God can be a mother to the motherless. I never had a chance to apologize to my friend Marvelous. God also stated in the Bible that "I am." This means he can be anything we need. A mother is a nurturer, a caregiver, and for some, affectionate. God our father can be all these things. I was both wrong and right. See, I told you earlier I was petty. Yes, being devoted to your faith is worth something. If you are persistent and genuine and pray honestly and faithfully, then God hears you. What happens when you pray, and you don't get exactly what you ask for? Everything is for a reason applies even when God says no. Since I was young, single, and fit, I heard I could pray and ask God for what I wanted. This time I was not taking any chances. I created my wish list for finding a husband. I chronologically listed features and traits a man must have to become my potential husband. Check out my prayer below.

Lord, I'm asking you for a husband. Please let him have the following things:

1. Let him be tall, dark, and handsome.
2. Let him have a car that's his own.
3. Let him have his own bank account.
4. Let him have one or no children.
5. Let him be college educated.
6. Let him be physically fit.
7. Let him genuinely like and learn to love my daughter.

These are the prayers I set before you, Amen.

Now this may not seem like asking for too much, but I had to edit this list at least a few times. I kept it in my drawer to update it as needed and then to manifest it. Going off topic for a bit I had a lady associate tell me how she was manifesting herself a husband. On New Year's Eve, she told me that she would sit and eat grapes in red lingerie. She says she was told to eat twelve green grapes on New Year's Eve then supposedly she's going to receive an engagement offer from someone that year. I'll have to get back to you guys on this because she never went through with it. I will need to check with other women or sources to see if this came true for anyone. Shout out to Kris and all the women out there who are looking for love and to be married.

CHAPTER 7

TIME IS OF THE ESSENCE

Today's generation is not the same. People are not putting an emphasis or priority on marriage itself. This is a sad idea because marriage creates strong families. Black and Brown families need not lose this practice. Today casual dating, promiscuity, and this new concept of co-parenting is taking over. I think we are losing something in this. Being so carefree and intimately engaging, so many people leave us used and often unfulfilled. The gratification felt is only temporary and fleeting. In some circumstances, I can understand co-parenting, but our kids still miss out on experiences. There is an experience from growing up with both parents in the same household that is positive. It often also creates a sense of unified discipline and discussion when two parents live together in a household with their children. This also helps our kids see what it is like for parents to work through disagreements and how to problem solve together.

Marriage makes a woman and a man accountable to their vows to each other and to God. Young people out there, it is still good to marry. Choosing the right partner is key and to be able to make the correct decision I would say pray. Pray often and pay attention to the signs around you and the Holy Spirit within you. If you're single, then that's no problem, enjoy your life and try to keep your body pure and holy. We are human and we do fail. We do at times get weak and get tempted. If you fail, it does not mean you are lost. Just get up and try again to do the right thing.

While I was on this journey, I would find guys that would have four out of five of the things on the wish list but never all. I expanded the list to add about ten more things. Then I heard a crazy concept in my twenties about the eighty:twenty rule. It was explained to me that no one in life will have 100 percent of what you need. Because we're human, we never could be 100 percent perfect. Only God can. Due to this, one should be happy to settle with someone who had 80 percent of what they were looking for. If they did, then they could overlook the 20 percent of what they felt was missing in wanting a partner. I would say today, though, if you found someone with most of the items on the list, this might be a winner. It could be somewhere between 75 to 80 percent or more.

Then like a brick dropped out of a construction site it hit me! I have someone who meets the eighty:twenty-rule requirement. So that settles it. I'm ready for a husband. My number one candidate was a good friend and personal fan of mine. Smiley was the one on the top of my list. We spent many days and nights for a few years talking over the phone. Then one holiday during a surprise visit he popped the question. I was grateful and accepted but I also panicked. Alright enough suspense, so I would say yes. Still, don't think that I was agreeing to marrying tomorrow. I hope not?

When is the right time to marry? The thing is, there is no right answer to this question. Once you feel you are ready, then you should. The Bible talks about how we should keep ourselves unto God. However, if this flesh is tempting you, and I'm paraphrasing, it's better to marry than to burn from sexual immorality. Whew! That was heavy. I have read that Hell is hot and if you don't believe it's true and you end up there, then God speed! I have no desire to burn and be tortured indefinitely, so I will do all that I can to be make it to Heaven with Christ.

Now we move on to the brothers, and don't get mad at me when you read this part. Here is a revelation for you folks. A man can get married and procreate for a much longer window than a woman can. As women, we have between puberty and before menopause for childbearing. Ladies who wish to get married cannot afford to waste time. In my opinion, an optimal time for a woman to marry is between twenty-two and thirty-two. For those that can't count that is a short period of about ten years. Meanwhile men can procreate from their teens to almost around their eighties. Just give some about a 50 here window to create life. Karma seems unfair, right? Maybe but this is subjective, it depends on how you look at it. Being pregnant and having a child is an exceedingly demanding thing to do. It is my belief that most older women would not want to do this unless there was some weird circumstances involved.

I am a science major who has worked over twenty-five years in healthcare. I would prioritize a woman having a safe delivery and healthy baby over a long tenure of years to have children. In this world I believe you are blessed to be here. If you can create even one life and that life surpasses your own, you are highly blessed. While I stoop down again to *Kiss my Cross*, it reminds me of my humanity. I am truly blessed to exist in this world and know that so many babies never made it here. This humbles me to thank Father God for creation (myself) and the Creator (Christ) entering this world for me.

With this is in mind we should always remember to do all that we can do, while we can. To present ourselves as our best version here on the Earth while we exist. To reach someone who is in a dire situation or who is without faith to point the way to God. I understand that some people here on Earth will never procreate and that is ok. They may stay forever childless, or some may even adopt. The goal is to maximize our time here to do all the good we can do while here on this planet. Now, baby, what they do on the other planets I couldn't even tell you!

CHAPTER 8

LET'S TALK ABOUT MISTER M

Now we are getting to the good part so let's talk about Mister M. Mr. M and I have been acquainted now for a few years. Marriage is the M and if you find yourself wanting to take the plunge, then just know that getting married and staying married are two different things. Marriage itself is a simple ceremony often performed in front of guest and clergy after people have previously applied for applications to enter this bond. The ceremony is fun and a lot or a little planning filled with emotions, creativity, and joy. Baby, this is only temporary for a day. After the ceremony and moving forward marriage is a work in progress. Some people say it's a piece of cake and others would say it's hard labor. I have been married seventeen years now and would call it a "labor cake."

Yes, I am a thick Black girl and I do like myself a good slice of cake. Marriage is a labor of love. It is like a baker who would put in many hours of fine ingredients then delicately layer, apply icing, and then decorate the most beautiful cake. It can be both sweet and satisfying and a lot of work. What it does is urge us to care for our partners' needs and sometimes before our own. It requires you to be selfless to a degree. If you see marriage in your future yield to the tips I have listed below:

1. Love and if fails, then allow yourself to love again.
2. Know your spouse and anticipate sometimes to meet their needs and surprise them sometime.
3. Don't say those vows and not mean them!

4. Hold yourself accountable all the time.

5. Spend time together and often.

6. Spend time separately to use that to focus on God and yourself.

When it comes to marriage, most people figure out that they want the ceremony and not so much the lifetime together. This is why parties are so big in our society. People love to host baby showers and throw gender reveals but not enter marriage. Today's adults even would prefer co-parenting over marriage.

Never fear, though, someone still wants to be married. Don't you let this world trick you into upholding your standards. If you're single and celibate, stay holy! And if you're single and you're sometimes celibate aka half-i-bant, stay prayerful. OK, I know that wasn't a real word, laugh out loud. This was slang for someone who isn't perfect, who has had sexual experiences, regretfully, and who is looking but still hasn't found a spouse. Not that the sexual experiences were not flesh fulfilling, but they were not permanent. Therefore, if you're a hoe-male or female, repent. (You get it, stop acting like that.)

Girl, I feel like I just closed the sermon. My point in all of this is to tell someone not to lose hope. God can bless someone who isn't perfect. He can use us when we are good, half good, or not good at all. This brings me a lot of light in my heart. To all my friends out there, I want you to remain hopeful. In our nastiest, haughtiest, most vile and dirtiest self, God can use and recreate you.

CHAPTER 9

A NEW THING

It's called a new beginning. Trust me, I thought about creating a fashion clothing line just for this purpose. The purpose is to encourage people, to point them towards God, and to remind them to never give up. Elohim, the name of the creator God, can restructure us. I know to our finite human minds this can be confusing. I was this-years- old when I learned that God had so many different names. OK, to be truthful, I learned it back a few years ago. I put myself at that time into an intense study to finding out some of the names of God back in 2022. I found the list of over a few years ago which each name depicted a different characteristic of God. This is utterly amazing that God has so many unique features and aspects. It really is mind blowing.

Creator God reminds me of the Lego expert builder. He is the architect and engineer of our lives here while on Earth. Many people are aware of this, and some are not. We can take inspiration from our creator. This allows us to creatively and artfully use skills given to us to become our own version of expert builders. A few of us in the top percents of society build vastly in this world. Many in this group go on to be the top earners in the world and what we would call "masters." Hence today there is such a thing as an expert class for someone in expertise level teaching classes to those who wish to gain experience.

Now as we build in this world, we will have challenges and often. Sometimes evil and hatred comes to try to tear us apart. We may crack or become disconnected but we can be repaired. I just want to thank God for crackle. This is not my term so let me give credit to the Lego movie first. Crackle is the leftover pieces you have when your life or situation is falling apart. When life deals you a crumbling hand, there is a repair to fix your situation, and that fix is able by the help of the Holy Spirit. It is the essence of God like Crazy Glue that keeps us bonded and intact. In other words, Gorilla Glue has nothing on it! Trust me, I know all glues are not the same. There is Elmers's glue for kids' project and glue for gorillas. There is even nail and wig glues and glue sticks for your crafting projects.

Respectfully, each glue made is built to hold things in that class it was created for. God's glue AKA the spirit holds us together, and it fortifies us. He keeps us bound to God via our inner spirit man or woman. OK, here is a little disclaimer for you all. I grew up in the eighties and nineties. We had limited entertainment, so we found enjoyment in other ways to occupy our time. To my generation, Elmer's glue was like a skin care product. We spend time pouring our glue into our palms until it dried by blowing our breath over it, then spent time peeling it off our palms and rolling it into balls.

Now I don't know what the purpose of that was. What I do know is after that glue treatment our palms felt softer and smoother. Did our parents beat us for wasting the school glue? Absolutely. Knowing today about skin care I felt like that could have qualified us for an early skincare product. Today's youth are so fortunate to have so many skincare and beauty stores and even able to purchase products online. You spoiled brats, move over. Auntie wants to order some stuff too.

This I feel is what happens to us Geminis. We love being into a variety of different things and all at the same time. This is how I sometimes get off topic. The takeaway AKA the gag is to go out daily and make choices. OK, just continue to create. Build the beings that excite your life and inspire you. Touch lives while doing it and solve others' problems when you can. Then when you make a mistake, having God in your life can get you back on track. He only requires that we confess and seek after him. When you find you do make a mistake and being human, you will, ask God to forgive you and get you back in good standings. Notice how I said when you make a mistake and not if. In a perfect world we would have perfect people doing all things well and never failing, but that doesn't exist. On Earth, no human is perfect. Even at our best versions of ourselves, we fail. We make mistakes, and we miss the mark. I had to learn this the hard way that I am not perfect. I do strive to be better daily. I am a flawed person that needs to evolve, do work. I am quick to point out other people's mistakes and not always ready to own up to my own. I may let another person get by after making a mistake but if you openly burn me then I would put you in your place. Jesus does not want us to be like that, I know.

OK, so let us go into detail. If someone smacks you on the cheek thinking because you love God, you are a coward, they are going to get the fight of their lives. Trust me, I am going to open a can of Psalms and I used that word for purpose of not telling you how I would be whopping them. I know that Mrs. Obama told us when people go low, we are to go high. One of my managers one day told me, "When people go low, we are supposed to go to Hell." In my heart I really do like it and agree but the God in me tells me that I am supposed to do the opposite of this and be better. I know that being a Christian requires me to walk like Jesus would. Keep praying for me because I have not ironed this down 100 percent. If the above happened to me, I would probably press charges on the person and consider catching them later outside. (Ok, just joking.)

In the Bible, my role model, Peter, sliced off ears and cursed people out, amongst other more positive things. Notice how we as humans are always looking at and recognizing the naughty things people do. It's like learning a second language and using all the cuss words first. He too was the Lord's servant and was innovative and slightly gangster, but without him the Gentiles would have not been reached. He was a fisher by skill and was multilingual. Peter was well versed. He was one of the close members of Jesus's inner circle. In many ways he reminds me of myself: skilled, creative, and feisty. I love Peter and one day when I make it to Heaven, I want to give him a high five. Please, Lord, just allow me and Peter to have this one moment in Heaven without anyone getting kicked out. Amen!

I know many people have their personal favorites when they read the Bible. Many of those saints include Mary, Abraham, and John. Peter was by far one of my favorites because he was relentless.

Why I like Peter so much is because I can relate to him. As a fisherman and a captain, he worked with his hands and did physical labor. His faith was also greater than others as he was extended additional amenities. Don't blame me, I had to use the word you relate to. Most of you travel on vacation so you're familiar with being rewarded with exceptions. Jesus made an exception and allowed Peter to even walk on water. Say what you want about my guy, Peter, but how many of you have walked on the water? Another reason I love Peter is because he was not afraid to cry out for help. People share no empathy for us who are strong. When you are strong, they expect you to be that way always and never have a weak moment. The Devil is a liar. When I am weak, God is strong.

My friend Peter demonstrated weak moments like when he denied Jesus three times. He also had a weak moment when he gave into violence and cut off the ear of a servant sent to arrest Jesus. I also have many weak moments. In life we are expected to put the weight of stress sometimes on our shoulders and bear it like Jesus. Well to this I say no. Jesus told us to take up our crosses and follow him. However, for our heavy burdens he told us to cast them on him because they would become light. Here is a free golden ticket for you all. Asking for help is OK. If we can't find him to confide in, then we can go and ask God for help. To me help is an acronym for: hey, emergency, Lord, please. This is much like a spiritual SOS. Psalms 120 says, "I cried unto the Lord, and he heard me." Thank God for that.

CHAPTER 10

WHAT SHALL I RENDER?

Don't run away yet my friends. Render is a fancy word for give. There is a Christian hymn that asks what we should render? The answer is easy, people, just like the multiple-choice tests we had as children. The answer is C (duh). Ok, not actually, it is our heart, our will. God wants us to surrender our hearts and our will to him completely.

I know you worry that I'm lost again but I assure you I am right on track. Today the church that I attend teaches abundant living. We are told when it comes to God, we could give our time, talent, energy, gifts, and money. This shows us that there is more than one avenue in which you can be used by God and bless others. How then do I give my time? That's simple, OK. I give my time by reading the Bible and meditating on the word. I participate in a weekly Bible study and four or so times a week write down personal tips from sermons heard. I research scriptures in the Bible that give me tips on living and how to apply to my own life. I spend time talking with my family about God and the people I work with and even to my social media friends.

To whom much is given much is also required. I feel that God spends time depositing into each of us talents and gifts. For me, I feel my gifts are in healthcare, fashion, and the arts and then empathizing. I've been a healthcare employee for over twenty-five years. How many years have I felt fulfillment with taking care of people's health? It has been all of them. Fashion is one of my first loves besides baked goods. I love to create and express myself. I love to paint, draw, sing, and sew fashion. Music is my second love after fashion. I love the expression of sound and exploring different genres. Since I was a child, I would listen to music secretly in the bathroom while getting in trouble taking too long to get ready. I feel like God created my heart differently. In my belief this is modeled after my late father. He grew up quickly in an exceptionally large family of over fourteen children and to him the more people you love the better you are in life.

Dad demonstrated to me what kindness was and how to model it. Today I'm a better person and I think a better Christian because of it. He taught me to care for others and have a sensitivity to make things better for other people not just focusing on myself. He was the greatest demonstration of what patience looked like for me. The older I get, the more I try to model my life around this. I like to give people grace even though they may not deserve it and to use my patience just as I would want someone to use for me.

CHAPTER 11

HALF-AND-HALF

After reading the title of this chapter, I bet you think you know where this is leading to. Young people under twenty may not identify with this. Let's get this out the way and say it out loud so we can move forward. My name is Lynette and yes, I like coffee! What I like best about it is the cream and the richness of it. Remember in the beginning of this story I told you how I like options. Half-and-half is a type of milk consisting of part cream and part milk. When drinking a cup of coffee with half-and-half it's all about the ratio. Now let's take this formula and apply it to my life. I, Lynette, am very much like half-and-half. I am half from the hood (part ratchet) and half Holy and classy. Trust and believe that my spirit commands me to do, say, and even act right. Thank goodness because my flesh wants me to cuss at some folks, stomp a mudhole in others and open a large can of common sense on the rest. Now I've learned to not be led by my feelings. I may have them, but I will not let them have me. I am the queen bee in control.

We are spirit beings living in a soul that inhabits a body. I have submitted and given my spirit to God. My soul is complex and is a collection of my emotion's thoughts and memories. Emotions are both high and low and thoughts can be good or bad. Memories can be happy, sad, hurtful, or a combination of all the things we've experienced. In my soul lies all the things that uniquely make me myself. My body is flesh but it is also my house for the inner parts of my being. It is the temple of the Holy Spirit.

To make a long story short I am a work in progress. Although now I am aware that every individual alive is also the same. We are here on this Earth taking a life walk. Every day we live in this three-part person we live, love, and even lie. The difference is to try and make the attempt to do right, be right, and live right. We are not perfect though and we fail. Falling short of these goals we sin and even sabotage others and ourselves daily. Humanity is by far a great creation but by God's standards we fall short.

Let's get into what makes me. Moving forward we'll get to the juicy parts. Today I am one of those semi preppies and sometimes dainty sisters. That is when I'm not listening to hip hop and threatening to bust someone in my family's head open but only in thought. In my human mind I try to justify how God knows who I am and what I am like because he made me. He knows I like to fly and drink wine and every now and then have an occasional cocktail. Now you know and I know that is not right 100 percent. God is holy. He requires us to be holy and if anyone tells you anything else, they're lying. If I'm going to tell the story, then I must remain honest with you. This doesn't mean that I am perfect, and I will tell you that I am not.

What it does mean is that I am aligning myself to the virtue and attributes of God. That means often to put down that third glass of wine. (Did I say third? I meant second.) Let me say something here, though, and it is that daily we must try to do and be good. Build up your faith by reading a Bible for yourself. Just take one step and then the other, just like riding a bike, and before you know it, you will be on the right path. As you make your way down this path, and you look over and see me traveling parallel give a girl a shout out.

CHAPTER 12

NARROW VS WIDE

In today's culture people think that wide is better. We have these trucks with wide back bodies, and we have these women with wide butt implants. We have people with veneers and not all of them but some have these great oversized white teeth. In spirit context, the Bible states that the wide gate leads to Hell. No thank you. In this world people are focused on the broadest, biggest, finest, and most flamboyant things to have and to love and to chase after. How many people are motivated by the love of money? The Bible teaches that the love for money is the root of all evil. This does not mean we don't need it, or shouldn't obtain it, and as Christians shouldn't multiply it. Let the church say Amen, pass the collection plate to your left.

Listen to the Biblical instruction. It states the way to heaven is a narrow gate. Now tell the truth: How many people do you know if they had a choice would pick a narrow path to go down? Just think of it in terms of a narrow bridge for a narrow landing, or even a narrow chance of survival post-surgery. Narrow to people just does not sound good. It makes me think of narrow width shoes. If you have narrow feet, please forgive me, but I just wouldn't want to be forced to submit to this.

We must recondition how we think. If something is narrow, then it means there is still opportunity for it to be or exist. Narrowing something down also excludes a number of unnecessary choices. Just because something is narrow doesn't exclude that it is still a choice. Think about someone with a narrow waist who can easily fit into so many options. Or being considered in a narrow round of candidates for a high-ranking position. I think narrowing down on this helps us to be more focused on the options we have.

This is a good thing, and we must evolve our thoughts. God reminds us that his thoughts are higher than ours. When we home in and narrow our thoughts and mind on God we are walking in his path. As a human this is a process our whole lives while on Earth. This is known as sanctification. First, we receive justification by faith in God. Then we walk this walk of Christianity our whole life while here trying to be the best version of ourselves. Today, it's much like the famous people who often are re-branding and somewhat transforming their images to the public.

CHAPTER 13

HIS GUIDING LIGHT

Excuse me, who turned the lights on in here? One day, I had a vision of Jesus standing in a room with me and he was so bright that I couldn't make out his image, but I knew it was him. Now let us put this into context. I was sick at this time, at twenty-three, in the hospital fighting off an infection. Stopping to eat in a deli in Upstate NY while visiting my sister, I became severely ill just twenty-three or twenty-four hours after eating a sandwich. I was quickly ill and had been hospitalized, suddenly getting sick. I had contracted bacterial meningitis, and it was very serious, and I was very ill. May I just say that at the times you are down is when it feels that's when the enemy Satan attacks you.

I was petitioned while in the hospital to appear in court to fight a custody battle for my then fourteen-month-old daughter. I was admitted for stay and scared as it was my first-time being a patient for a lengthy stay in a hospital. I was there for about one week. The hospital arranged a team of specialists to come manage my care and try to heal me. If I can just say this, first I want to give an honor to God, the head of my life, and my savior the Lord Jesus Christ. I know it's not an award ceremony but thank God this was the bacteria kind and not the viral brain-eating kind.

My parents kept and took care of my daughter that week while coming to visit me. The bacteria were starting to affect my knee and unbelievably my vision. I had severe bouts of high fevers, achiness, and extreme headaches. Yes, the father of my child was taking me to court for a custody battle. To me, it didn't make sense because he left me so often alone to care for her. I had my parents help me petition the judge for an extension. In the meantime, I laid in my hospital bed and cried and then I prayed.

Now you all might say it was the fever and that I was seeing things, but I said it was God. It was amazing that while I was there, I had two strangers offer to pray for me who were hospital employees that simply worked where I was. The janitor's husband she said was a minister, and she dialed a number on my phone to have him pray for me, so he did. On another occasion, my housekeeper, who was Catholic, offered to come over and pray for me and we did together. Some days after these people prayed, I would finally be released just a day before my court appearance. People, let me tell you this, God hears our cries and our prayers. I lay in the dark that night and so I was having difficulty seeing and having great sensitivity to the lights in the room. Just then a white figure walked into my room, came over to my bed, touched me, and then disappeared into the corner.

That same evening while making his rounds the doctor informed me I would be released that same day, and my parents could pick me up. I still was not seeing well but would be able the next day to make my court date and fight for my daughter. I went home and when I got there my mom took me to church and that day, she brought me up before the altar and the church elders and they prayed over me.

At this point, my vision was turning, and I could now see limited shapes and colors. The next day I went to court with my Bible in hand. The same Bible I had been meditating over and in for the last fourteen months since having my baby. My ex never knew how sick I was then— didn't know I was in the hospital or at the moment temporarily couldn't even see well. While in court that day we were both awarded joint custody of my child, but I was given sole primary custody as her mom. At the time I was mocked by him, the father, who at the time was angry and laughed at my face as he stared me down with my Bible. I kept the faith though, and I went home that day with my baby in my hands. It took me about three days more after one of the hardest fights of my life to recover fully.

I realize today that God sent people to pray for me and then he touched me. Although I was weak at the time, I needed to be strong, and I found favor because I relied on him and because of it I had victory.

Growing up my parents liked to watch soap operas. My mom's favorite story was one of many popular daytime soap operas. I never got into soap operas. There was always too much going on for me. I find it amazing because today I love watching K dramas and or African Nollywood drama shows. One thing her show reminds me of is to follow the path that God leaves for us. He knows the plans he has for us, and they are good. We only must be willing to submit our will and follow the steps.

Myself, I am hardheaded. My grandmother would say my head was "like a rock." Lord, I know that I am aggie or what is known as an abbreviation today for aggravating. Still could you please shine your beams of light in this direction? If possible, can you set off a set of LED lights for me? Your daughter down here is just distracted too easily. I know syndromes like ADD exist, but I never was diagnosed with that; however, I told you I get distracted easily and I am a Gemini. I am told that people born in this month get involved in multiple things all at the same time.

It is important that I ask and request of God to do this for me. If not, I will end up somewhere off the path. As I grow in maturity, though, I do know I also have to take accountability, and I pray the Lord lead me down the right path. Or I may end up somewhere lost, shopping or getting some kind of self-care service. I am so glad that our father is patient and not easily swayed like me or us humans. The mercy that God shows me keeps me close to the cross within kissing distance. I am ever mindful that I need to carry my load and walk the path of the road the way Jesus has led me to.

CHAPTER 14

TAG, YOU'RE IT

If you grew up here as a teen in America, you know this game. Tag is a game in which one person was designated as "it." Every other person would run and hide while "it" and not the clown would do a count down from ten to zero. After the countdown that person would be set free to chase people until they found them. Once they caught them, they would be free, and the caught person had to take the chaser's place. Focus a little closer on the idea of a tag. A tag is in definition a label attached to someone or thing for the purpose of identification. Be it freeze tag, nametag, luggage tag or label tag, each one has a specific identity. Here is a small little caveat about when you first accept Christ. (Tag, you're it!)

Yes, at first you get this great feeling of endorphins that makes you proud and happy that you chose Christ. This is a good start, don't think otherwise. In time you become a living, breathing, and walking target of the enemy. My friend's darkness and the forces of evil take notice of this and somehow put an unseen most-wanted tag on your back. My advice for this is to stay in prayer and keep close to God. Though you may be a target if you stay in God and keep close, you will stay kept. The Bible talks about how no weapons formed against us will prosper.

Boy, this makes your sister thankful because my Kung-Fu is only in my imagination or on TV. I do still have a small trace of the physical ability to lay a smack down, but this is not the right way to fight. Brace yourself. If you are a fighter like me, I know you didn't like that last sentence and neither did I. We must fight evil, enemies, and Satan with the Word. Not our word but rather using the word of God that was written in the Bible. There are also other tools to keep evil at bay. Pray to God daily and often, developing it into a daily routine and never quit.

As a matter of fact, God said to pray to him in all things, with thanksgiving to Him, of course, and let our requests be made known. Now me I tend to think that I surely can't bother God with all things because that would be silly, right? I don't know how I am supposed to answer that. Just imagine me saying, "Jesus, I am out of coffee for my Keurig today. Please help me find instant coffee somewhere around this kitchen for my co-workers and for my boss to get the business today. Amen." Nope. I will not do it! I will not waste the good master's time like this. When I pray, I am intentional on what I want to interrupt God with, to bring to his attention to help me with. I still pray daily a few times a day about different things. You better believe me, though, I will not waste a prayer on something I know that I can do, change, or fix myself.

The way my brain is wired is a little different from some people and I just want to warn you of this. I ask the Holy Spirit to get involved and to tag Jesus in on this to get this request straight into the hands of Father God. In many ways prayer reminds me of a four by four relay. I pray and pass the baton to the Spirit, and he moves it into the hands of Christ. Jesus then takes that petition and hurls it into the arms of the Father. Just like that, is how I think. Praying reminds me of the 400m hurdle. In which I am at first fast but after a few hurdles barely strong enough to clear my leg of the race. As I stride in prayer, barely clearing the tops without disqualifying, then casting all my hope and trust in the rest of the team who would help us place.

The good news is that with God you are on the winning team. No matter how it looks or feels in the end you are victorious. This is the best news of all so don't faint during the race. The race is a challenge. It's steady and vigorous but with the right team you will succeed. Here is a tip, though. In a relay, there is no success on your own. Here is that part where people roll their eyes, I know, and it involves being a team player. There is no I in team as we have all heard. This is the truth also

58

in Christianity. Together all of God's people make up the church, one unified body. There is strength in unity, and we need fellowship with one another. Today, there are so many people who feel alone and depressed and this is when the enemy has a door he can seep into. Alone we are isolated, and, in this way, we are an easy target in tag.

We recognized that as children playing. When the person who was chosen to be it would come after one of us alone, we would run into groups of several people together. It was harder to get caught by that one person when there were many people standing together. To make a long story short people need other people.

CHAPTER 15

DUCK, DUCK, GOOSE

I know at this point you are sick of me but after this chapter we will get back to grown folks' territory. Do you ever wonder, like me, why God created people in so many colors and ethnicities? I believe the Creator is an artist, like me. We may have DNA we get from our genetics of both parents, but we all have an individual style. In the world today people live their lives following the latest trends. We see this on social media, on TV, and in our music. The world sets parameters for people which make them believe they must fit into a certain category. I don't believe in following such trends. I know that God made me an individual with extremely specific qualities, tendencies, and features. In fact, I believe he created every human being this way, even twins and people born with multiple births.

There is something significant about you that not anyone could do just the way you do. We leave a certain mark on the world made by the person we are here. Not all birds are created equally. A duck is a member of the bird species but is different from a goose.

One interesting science fact I just found out while drafting this book is that some species of ducks are omnivores while most geese are herbivores. When I think of a duck, it reminds me of many days of seeing a mother duck walk across a parking lot with all her babies behind her in a row.

Each one follows the bird in front of them and barely steps out of line. Then I think of a goose which you see flying overhead at times in patterns or individually making a whole lot of commotion.

In our faith journeys, we should be as disciplined as a baby duck and as adventurous as a goose. Being a Christian requires that we learn and practice often to stay disciplined. The Bible says how God is all about decency and order. We must, and this includes me, learn to obey the Word of God and to obey when he speaks to us individually. It sounds hard, but it is simply a matter of keeping ourselves in line and accountable.

To be a goose requires that you fly high and float on the water. Geese are smart enough to know when the climate changes to migrate. As Christians we should be constantly living and functioning on a frequency above that of the world standards. We should be following the Word of God and listening while watching for changes that indicate it's time for us to shift. People are afraid of making changes for fear of losing something they think may be good. I had to learn to welcome change on my path of Spiritual Growth. On my faith journey I want to remain pliable and flexible like those thin little skinny yoga people on YouTube. In my ability to do so I can expand and move like God does. That is right, you heard me. God is a Spirit, and He is a moving, speaking, Lord. Now, throw away the idea of fearing change all ye introverts. I did. Grab your stretch leggings and break out your mini microphones and let's get to work.

I own a couple of bamboo plants that I bought at my local store. I have had them for five years now and they have grown substantially. There are days I spend enjoying looking at them. One of my favorite things about them is that they bend and bow but do not break. They continue to be strong and push higher. Sure, they have some leaves that turn yellow on each plant that I prune back a couple times of year. My amazement always lies, though, in how resilient they are and continue to flourish. It reminds me of myself.

My friends and family life will throw you an array of situations to deal with. We must be like ducks, geese, and bamboo. Remain disciplined as a duck following the leader. Christ is our leader and we are his followers. Be resistant to follow in the way of the world, not having to live by the status quo. It will be hard, but you will be the standard. We may trim at certain times like pruning but keep growing. When you must be moved from side to side go with flow, but don't you cave in the wind. The trees bough and bend and so do mighty flowers. Notice I said when and not if because in life you will experience some hardship. If you have never yet experienced any hardship in life, then I leave you with a saying my late grandmother shared with me: "Keep living."

CHAPTER 16

YOU SNOOZE, YOU LOSE

As a young girl growing up, I loved to sleep in late. I would spend hours at home daydreaming and planning in my young mind what I thought a perfect life would be. Then sometime later as a young adolescent, I imagined that I knew what the perfect career and family would be like. I didn't know about doodle squat then. Yep, I said that. Today I am aware that dreaming can be productive if focus into the right direction. I have since childhood dreamed about meeting God and having him either come save me, tell me something, or show me something to come. We all need rest while we reside in these human bodies. There is a difference, however, between rest and being lazy. In our period of deep rest R.E.M. our minds and bodies are recalibrated, reach equilibrium, and in this are rejuvenated. Lying around being lazy and expecting good things to come for you in life is a fairy tale. In fact, we grow up hearing tales of how if we lay up in wait we will be rescued. This is not the reality of life. It may be certain cases in which a person is rescued like a medical emergency or a parent or adult rescuing a child. In most circumstances, though, we must do the work to get the outcome we imagine or dream of. In some cases you may have more of an advantage in which things are laid up for you to succeed such as God has already planned. My calendar planner for this year quotes an important quote from the book of Jeremiah.

"For I know the plans I have for you, to prosper you and not harm you. Plans to give you hope and a future." For me this sets the tone of how to live my life forward. It tells me that God has multiple plans for me because this word is plural not singular. Next, he planned that what I have is financially successful and that I am flourishing growing strong and healthy. What I can say is that in this life you should dream. If you thought I wouldn't say that then you were wrong, I am keeping this book real. I dream of things I want to achieve and of childhood dreams from my past that I put off.

After being a wife and raising two children and growing in maturity, I am at a point where I can now put my dreams first. When you love, you sacrifice for those that you love. At times so much so that we put their needs and wants sometimes before our own. We live out our lives trying to provide stability, values, and direction for our children and families. Most of us do but in caring for our loved ones we sometimes put ourselves last. Women are known to do this more so than men. In many ways after a woman has either raised her children or reached a certain age of maturity it is then she decides to go live her best life. For some people, this stage of making our dreams come true happens at the halfway mark of our lives. Why, wait? I say screw that and live each day with purpose and to the fullest. Stop putting your alarm clock on snooze and get up and do something today. Take notice, I did not say don't put on your alarm. You will not sit here and blame me for being late to work, Sis. Dream then record what you have seen. Meditate on it then make it happen, captain!

Most importantly, if you get a thought don't wait too long to act on it. When I was seventeen, I came into a few thousand dollars due to a personal injury. At that time, I thought of investing it in Dunkin because I would stop by daily for a donut, newspaper for twenty-five cents and a fifty-cent coffee. I thought I should have put that money in stocks because this one day would become popular. Boy was I a big dummy because I missed buying stock like I thought I should have in this company at that time. In the past I have thought of items for household cleaning and then looked around to see someone else having developed the item. In other times I have thought of creating a certain type of fashion item and waited and someone else created the very thing. I could be wrong, but I think God downloads us certain things to champion or produce in this world and if we don't, he moves on and gives the idea to someone else.

Today in this twenty-first century I do not want to miss any Word of God, even a dream that I am to fulfill. I am fine tuning my hearing and sight but also my spirit and my discernment so that I don't miss what I am to do here. Living here on Earth is like living our lives backwards, forward. I know that was a bit much but maybe you can visualize it this way. God has already created our lives and paths marked until its end. Then we come to this Earth and live out the path that was destined for us until we arrive at the End. Our path in life even allows for some divergence which is where God builds in added steps to get us to the desired outcome. This is quite amazing and at the same time unfathomable. As much as we know in this day with our human minds it is all childish to our father God.

I consider all the great developments today of humans in science and technology, in engineering and math, and it all is minor to the Master. We are like a little speckle of dirt in this great big atmosphere of life. Dust we are and trust me one day we also again become dust. There is a number that we can't see or know in each person's head that exists here on Earth. Use your number wisely my friends. You snooze then you lose and that is only on yourself.

CHAPTER 17

ME AND MY LIPSTICK

Now we are moving into another one of my favorite categories of expression: makeup. I can tell you today that I love makeup and for a girl who at one time couldn't see her "tomboy self" wearing it, I would blow your socks off today with a full face glam, (hah). It took me a little bit of experimenting to find what works for me. I love to frequent the makeup counters. I know I told y'all about how hot pink and red were off limits to us as young ladies. As a lady I can say that having the perfect lipstick color can make a strong impact.

What good would lipstick be without us having lips? Our lips function to hold food in our mouth and to close airtight. They help us to keep out unwanted objects and to even allow communication and to show emotion. Even as an introvert I have a bad habit as you know of getting to speak the last word. This isn't a good thing as sometimes there are things better not said. Our lips can help us be a guard for the things we should not speak. The Bible talks a lot about bridling your tongue and in today's translation I take that as, "Shut your you guessed it." We must control the things we say because our mouths can alter our situations. Have you ever heard quotes like, "Speak things into existence"? This is a real-life thing. When we speak, we must be careful not to speak evil or negatively, to not speak wrongfully against our families or friends unjustly. Not to even speak wrong about strangers.

My Bible tells me that the tongue is evil and restless and full of poison. The lips also are like a scorching fire. For that purpose, we are to put a guard over our mouths. In today's translation I would say lock it up! I am teaching this concept to my youngest child now and he is a teen. I tell him think twice on what He wants to say then speak only half of it. I want him to start now realizing that his words are meaningful and at times destructive. All of ours are the same as well. We must build up others when we speak and not tear them down. In school, teachers would say if you don't have anything nice to say then not to say anything at all.

As Christians we also must be selective on how we speak. God's word says to speak things that are not as though they are. This works perfectly in faith and when we are speaking of good things to come in our lives. A negative impact can happen though If we are not careful. If we start speaking doubt or not subduing and speaking bad thoughts or fear, we can create environments which are gateways to those things. So then do not dwell on these things. Think about the things that are lovely, pure, holy, and of good report. Think of the true and virtuous and honorable things. More importantly if you find you can't keep these things out of your mouth then shut your mouth. An effective way to keep your mouth closed is to apply a good coat of expensive lipstick. I promise you will not want to wear it off or smudge it up. You are also prone to smile more with those pretty lips. With a closed mouth you can still meditate to God. He can hear us when we are quiet and more importantly, we can hear him!

CHAPTER 18

ABIDE

Where you live isn't as important as being alive. As spirit beings, we are born into a soul that has a body which enters this world. Infants are brought home by parents or a parent to a dwelling place and this is where we live. A home is a place where we are cared for and protected and live as a member of a family or household. Home can mean different things to different people but most importantly it is a shelter. For me, a shelter is a place where we can come inside and be covered from the elements of the weather. In this place we are amongst company and for most of us it is where we are comfortable to let down our guard.

That's right, let your guard down, your girdle down, and if you have a bra or boxers on, then let them down too. In today's time we would tell you to let down your Spanx. Let down your wig and lashes and let your full face beat down. Refreshing, isn't it? Living in a relationship with God, being at complete rest to let down your guard and be authentic, is to abide. Today society wears a "faux" façade of who they really are just like they wear faux furs and leather. We often hide or shield the real versions of ourselves to protect ourselves from being harmed, mistreated, or being rejected. Under God's shield of formidable power there is no lack and no need for worry or anxiousness. These three are among the top troubles of this world and to be free from them is a relief.

Think back to a time in your life when you were carefree. When was this for your childhood? What do you find yourself doing when you are feeling the most relaxed? Keep in mind this is a Christian book so keep your thoughts in check, you little nasties. Just joking. Lack is a little bit different to pinpoint. Lack of what you need and what you want are two different things. If your basic needs are or have been met, then think of a time when you experienced this. I am aware that there are people in a better financial situation than others.

Some people have no lack in finances but lack in many other areas like love. You could be the wealthiest person in the world and still be lonely. You could also be the poorest person in the world and be rich with love and friendships. No matter where you find yourself on this spectrum you can have God in your life and be satisfied. If you have little, you can make it and if you have much, you can give more. Living in a constant state of relationship with God means you will always have a friend, a protector, a comforter. God will be better to you than a bestie, knocking out your enemies like Mayweather and cozier than them ugly Christmas pajamas. There, I said it! Now, you may want to know how is it that you are to abide? Great question. I have a little summary of steps below called Abide 101 in 2024:

1. Pray daily so you don't have to punch somebody's lights out…No so you act like the best version of yourself and not that bad version that tells you to do the crazy stuff.

2. Choose kindness, daily. Make decisions to bless those who do not deserve it. Remember in doing this we are reminded of how God gives us mercy we do not deserve.

3. Make someone laugh daily, smile, and bring joy when you enter a room. Let the atmosphere improve when you enter, and people miss you when you leave.

4. Stay in relationship with God. A relationship requires constant development and for us to give our time, energy, gifts, and talents.

5. Grow yourself. Expand in wisdom, knowledge, and knowing what God expects of us. Pick up the Bible and read daily. Meditate on the words like you would if you were studying at

the last minute for a test. For this new age generation, meditate on it like the number of followers you have on social media.

That's more than enough bullet points for you to have an idea of the way you should take. Now that you have a frame of how to remain in God we can wrap this thing up soon.

CHAPTER 19

THE HEART, A TREASURE AND TREACHEROUS

We have one heart and one life and if you have any favor here at least a chance of finding a true love while on Earth. Our hearts are amazing organs that help our entire body receive what it needs to function. Inside our hearts we store on an emotional level our deepest thoughts and desires. It is easy to set it up to receive love from someone we desire but it can also burn us. God is love and because of it he gave us hearts to experience the feeling for ourselves. Love is patient and kind. Love unreturned or revoked can also be an extremely dangerous and risky thing.

Love unrequited has started wars in past time. Love deferred makes the heart sick. Then what do you do when you love more than one person at a time? I am not God, I am his servant, so I do not pretend to know the correct answer to this. What I do know is that Father gives us the ability to love. Today I also know that there are several types of love. There is love like you would feel for a friend. A different type of love exists for a spouse, a sexual type of love. Then there is also a love you would feel for your deity, your God. I also know that having love and being in active love (yup, like a shooter) with someone is different. In our human existence we look for love and often amongst the people we are here with and not just from God. Looking for love can be a symptom of loneliness. In my experience when we go looking, we often end up finding friendships. The best love that I experienced happened when my lover came looking for me. In my situation I was holding on to a friend that I put in a position to be a lover but who wasn't looking for the same thing. At or around the same time, a lover came looking for me. In that person's eyes he had already held me in a special place where he relented to no one. Being ignorant and not really understanding what true love was at this time I felt I could accept both. I could keep the love of a friend who by default became a lover or accept the love of a man who wanted to love me for himself, genuinely. Why eat cake when you can have cookies too?

Boy was I dead wrong on this one. Until intimacy occurred, I could maintain a friendly relationship with both hearts. My heart felt like I could have both at the same time. Now, don't get crazy. I did not mean sexually but intimately in thought. I wanted to entertain attention from, talk, and hang out with both men. I was being greedy until at a certain point I had to "toss out the cookies." I was a young fool then. As much as I do like cookies, let me tell you firsthand, I would rather have cake! I chose to let go of the guy who showed genuine love for a man who only wanted sexual intimacy. In the end I was left with a broken heart full of envy for not choosing who I should have. That no good heart of mine wanted what she wanted, and she couldn't continue that way. The cookies turned out to be a big disappointment. It was like eating a dry hard cookie with no moisture. It was unfulfilling and undesirable other than a little sweet that wasn't memorable. I got exactly what it was that I deserved, a lesson! My lesson was to trust in God and stay holy and that when he saw fit, he would send someone to find me who would love me, and He did just that.

What I can advise to you from this lesson is to keep your heart pure. Don't entertain doing something you know is out of character and not like God. Trust that God has a good plan for your life and future, and he knows what you have need of. I needed a spouse, a true love who could hold me down and temper my anger and stubbornness. Today I know that I am blessed to have met and stayed with that person, my love. It also taught me to accept love from someone. Not to go attempting to falsely re-create it. Love is many things but most of all it is not fake.

For anyone out there ready to give in, I give you this word: keep going and don't quit; just abide. Live your life every day and include God in all your steps. Start by praying first thing in the morning and don't be embarrassed at first if it is short. The disciples (Jesus crew) aka gang-gang—OK, no, that's way too 2024 for me but they asked God to teach them how to pray and so should we. When I grew up, I would often watch people in church praying and worshipping, even testifying or praising, and wonder are these people faking this? Now with my adult knowledge of today I can assume the testimony part may have been true but some of the other ceremonial program not so sure of.

Remember, we said before only God can judge but it makes you question the authenticity of people. One thing I never wanted to do growing up was to fake I was in deeper with God than what I really was. I have too much respect to play around with God like that. I also learned that in church I need to focus and zone in on my own worship and praise and receiving the Word. This is why I come to God. Today my praise is authentic, and I am not ashamed of it. I do not feel like my praising God is forced because everyone around me is doing it. My relationship with God is genuine and natural. Now let's dig into my prayer life.

I am not the strongest or the weakest when it comes to my prayer life. I have been expanding on how to pray and to put things in order when I do. If I can be truthful to you, I will tell you I was out of order in prayer. I said it out of order and you're lucky I do not have a gavel! People like me, often come to God like he is Santa, a genie, or a leprechaun. We want to get a short prayer to him quickly where he turns around and solves our problems like a google search. No. God deserves more from us than this. Look at people of other religions prayer lives. Many often pray several times in one day and it hurts but we are guilty as charge we don't.

Our God wants to be included in all that we do, daily. We get caught up so often in our daily routine and family lives that we don't put him where he deserves on the throne. Just like people reverence a king, royalty, and emperor or president, how much more do we deserve to lift

GOD. We are not picking him up literally but worshipping Him with the awesome respect He warrants. If you are in question on how unexplainable God is, I recommend you read the book of Job. No cap, God reads Job like a kindergarten kid as he questions Job if he knows how creation is set and remains intact. Abba is truly impressive, indeed.

Go get your cup of soda and your bowl of popcorn and let's ponder this as I paraphrase. Get a bible and now follow me. Job 38 starts by saying, "Then the Lord spoke to Job out of the Storm." Excuse me? The first time I am outside, and the Lord speaks to me out of a storm I am not outside anymore. A little further God says, "Have you ever given orders to the morning, or shown the dawn its place, that it might take the Earth by the edges and shake the wicked out of it?" Excuse me, Father, I have placed orders in the morning at the fast-food spots and laid some edges on my own head, but this is out of my jurisdiction. Open the book and read it for yourself and it will help give perspective on how God's ways are not ours. Here is a way to develop your prayer life. First praise him and put him on his throne. Next ask forgiveness for your sins. Then ask for what you want in faith, believing you will get it. Don't forget to pray and expand on this format as you see fit and need.

CHAPTER 20

WRONG-WAY DRIVING

I know for all of us who drive or are pedestrians we have seen these different signs on the road. Caution and stop signs all over and safe crossing places like crosswalk signals and my favorite: Men Working. Clearly whoever created this sign didn't realize women are working too. But I digress, I understand this sign hopefully is meant to be inclusive. Many people have seen a dead-end sign or hospital sign with the big letter H. Who out there has ever encountered the Wrong Way sign? In life we can apply many of these traffic signs to how we are handling our lives, not just traffic.

Life can be joyous but also at times hectic. In my attempt to do my part to assist people with this I am creating a Christian streetwear line of clothing called Abide. I hope to reach people who are suffering in the world to point them to God. No matter what human emotion they are dealing with I am asking God to use me to help people recover. To encourage people who are without hope and lean towards giving in. Life is like a game of "Pac-Man." You find yourself running down your path and if you're moving in the right direction after a bit, you get rewarded by eating some fruit. Now this fruit is like a bonus. It is like a reward to eat an ice cream sundae or a delicious dessert or a reward food for me would be like a giant steak. Excuse me, that's just how my brain works. If you're moving too slow, you have a trail of enemies behind you waiting to devour you.

In many ways this game is like a demo of life. We are out here "running" our race of life moving along our path and every now and again stumbling on a good thing God leaves us which empowers us. As we get closer to our goal of clearing a level and moving to the next level of glory, the enemy gives chase. That no good enemy somehow finds numbers and all of them chase after you just like demons and wickedness chase after us Christians. I don't know if you recall this but in the event the enemy jumped you, the game gave you a new opportunity to reset and have a few chances of new beginnings. God is so much more merciful than this and he gives us many chances to begin new.

Dear Lord, it's your sis (ok, daughter) and I need a U turn sign ahead. If I am running on the wrong way, send me a sign. Help me and my pigeon-toed feet to the right direction. Lord put up a U-turn sign ahead and I won't be disappointed if I run up into an all-out stop sign. If the lane I am running in starts off good, but you see I need to divulge, sis will even be happy with a merge ahead sign. God feel free to encourage me with walking alongside good friendship with the pedestrians crossing sign. Father, I am grateful when you forewarn me of slippery road ahead and Abba when you want me to be attentive send me a traffic sign ahead. In Jesus' name I pray, and you guessed it…Amen

CHAPTER 21

I MUST GO ON

My dad passed away in 2006 just four months after I got married and I was at the age of twenty-nine. He was truly one of my favorite people in this world. Although I had some idea he may go because he had been sick, I felt so heartbroken when it did happen. I was distraught, and it took me several months to be able to tolerate him being gone. Then in 2012 my mother died. In her final days she fought with advanced heart disease and her pacemaker, and I felt it was a traitor. I will never forget my mom no longer being here.

God forbid you ever must see a pacemaker patient transition. I will never forget how she left this Earth and hope you never have to experience this. A pacemaker is a device surgically implanted under the skin on top of the heart to correct an abnormal rhythm. Well in the event a person experiences an irregular heart rhythm it delivers a shock to restore normal heart function. Let's just say during the final days of hospice my mom's pacemaker over-performed. That son of a biscuit (whew, pray for me I almost said it) was keeping her alive while it was also killing us, her loved one's watching, slowly. Why then did I call it a traitor? I will tell you. I studied pre-med in sciences and wanted to become a surgeon. I am an advocate for science but at the same time seeing it at work made me realize it works too well.

I decided I never want to be shocked by anyone or anything from then. I take solace in that my mother I know was a Christian and a firm believer in God. I knew that she may have been scared to leave behind the children she loved and the mother she was also the caregiver for, but we sent her home with closure. Her kids loved on her and in the end, we told her it was ok and that we loved her, and she could go on and rest. Within five days or so in hospice care, after two days of visiting with all her kids and most of her grandkids my mom went home to God. In retrospect, I know when it is your time to go you, my friend, are leaving the Earth. We were being greedy, wanting to keep our mother here longer than she was supposed to be. In hindsight my siblings and I learned our mother went in secret in 2006 to the hospital and had a pacemaker placed with no family present. She had at this time a sickly older spouse, a mother which she was the caregiver for, and four adult children and she went alone, but she wasn't alone. My mother went with God to that surgery, and it was successful, and it added six additional years of living to her life. She could have very well died the same year my dad did, but God.

This is my story and I hope to not bore anyone. Like me, you have lost someone you love to death. After you have cried and grieved and been depressed, what do you do next? Buckle up, this may be hard to hear but you must go on! Going on requires that you live and breathe and that you continue to do. I am a witness that life does go on and so can you. When you grieve after some while it is best to not be alone. My husband snapped me out of depression that I didn't realize I was entering into about four months after my mom has passed. It was his words that he shared, and I don't remember how it quite went but he told me to live on.

I know myself this is easier said than done. Don't get stuck in the feeling like you can't move forward, you can, and you will. If you need help doing so then get help. The key is to just start somewhere, one day. You may need to get a shower, wash up or clean your hair and give yourself grace to move forward. No one can charge you for loving them any less. Now, you must learn to live without them. Your love for them never truly leaves. It is my belief they are only physically gone and traces of them remain in your memories and your heart. How you go on is up to you, my friend. Some people create a memorial like a plaque or book a necklace or keep an article of their loved one's clothing. I did at first do these things and then I grew and became less selfish. I realized not to tie my family spirits down to this Earth and released most of the items that kept them dear in my heart. I know in my heart that my family members were saved spiritually and that they would end up in Heaven with God and loved ones.

One day we will reunite and at that point I will have taken my position of an Elder. In that day someone coming behind me will hopefully also be willing to release me to God. The spirit woman inside me will return to God. Then I will be made whole and presented to Jesus and have a big welcome party. At least this is in my imagination how it will go. In heaven God is on the throne so I may not get a whole party but just a party line intro with everyone would be fun.

Plants have the krebs cycle, animals have the animal kingdom, but humans have a life cycle. We start as a fertilized seed implanted in our moms until birth. From birth this baby grows into a child which later develops into an adolescent and finally into an adult. As adults grow older things begin to change. Adults grow into seniors who get weaker, slower, tired and eventually need help. Often as seniors age they need help like a baby would when it is young. Our bodies house a soul that contains a spirit which makes you yourself and this body returns to dust. Aye, Dios, mio!

We therefore have a goal to achieve in our life's journey. We are sent there to do the thing we were uniquely created for as God had planned. What someone else's life journey is I do not know. I know we would be unfulfilled if we were given this life to live and didn't meet the goal God set for us. If you admit defeat too soon, you may alter the plan or fall short. The straightforward way to solve this is to keep on going, and do you. You live life how you do as your genuine self is important here. Your journey may be necessary to aid or free someone else. Without you even being aware someone could be watching you and being strengthened by you. Wouldn't you want to pull them up by following the visual of your life lived? If they see you succeed and hear your story it may move theirs along.

Don't be selfish, you pay it forward and help the ones behind you. In doing this you are giving inspiration and encouragement to someone, and God loves a cheerful giver. I believe this to be true about our finances but also about other things. You can give a listening ear to someone on the brink of disaster or give a bit of laughter to someone who is feeling down. I want to help others and not just with money but with time, talent, and showing what the love of God feels like an adding a little humor. If I point you to God and you get on this train, you can pick up your cross and follow him like I am. The creator can heal and restore you and offer you a new beginning. All that no person could ever do for you he has done and will do greater.

When you are not even aware, he will do a new thing. Yes, my friends then you will be like that lady on social media in 2024 surprise, surprise. Next thing without thought you will turn around and lift someone and love them and the cycle begins again. My theory is that God put us here on the Earth to interact with one another that's why he created different genders and races. I think the goal here is to find out about him and spread the word so that we all can get back to him.

I am not ignorant and know that some people no matter what will not accept God. Some people are here and choose to be evil. That's their business and when they burn eternally, I hope they have a great love for Hell's flame and damnation of torture. Others I believe may not know they are headed that way or may have made wrong decisions but still may be redeemed. I think these people God put here to encounter someone else who will share the Word of his love and forgiveness through Christ and that person may have a chance. Even the goodie two shoes' people are here who have never done wrong and have a definite place in Heaven with no chance of missing the mark.

Think again, that is nonsense. Every living person has missed the mark, and all here are born in sin. Even if we are good humans, we are not perfect. Now let your shoulders down and relax. Even if you have made some mistakes, you still have a chance.

CHAPTER 22

REMEMBER ME

How do you want to be remembered? Humans are graced to be given a life and we strive to obtain and gain different things on our journey here. Many of the things we try to be remembered by are riches, power, fame, and worldly influence. When my life journey on Earth ends the thing, I want to be remembered by is to have loved God. Ater that my soul's achievement is for people to read into my life and say she modeled what God is like. In all that we do the most important thing to do is to honor and remember the Creator.

What is it that we do remember? I will tell you. We often in life can remember events that take place. Events like birthdays, graduations, a first kiss, or a marriage are often bookmarked in our minds and memories. Other events like childbirths, deaths of family members, or attending a favorite concert can also hold a special place in our hearts. We recall remembering good times and tough times. In fact, it is amazing all the things we lock into our heads to never forget. We were taught to remember our alphabet and math formulas and at one time to even memorize phone numbers. In my children's age they were taught to remember passwords and passcodes, pin numbers, and critical thinking. If that still isn't enough, kids of today are taught to remember memes, algorithms, cheat codes, and hacks.

The mind is truly an amazing thing. It is almost unfathomable the amount of information we load into our minds and the things we must retain daily. In all of that we serve little purpose if we remember all the above and more and do not remember our Maker. God wants us humans who are his creation to remember him. If you don't believe me, let me point out some things to you. If you ever go to a church often there is a table on the altar up front. Some of these are used for the purpose of receiving Holy Communion. Inscribed on the side of this table are often the words Do This in Remembrance of Me. (Uh-huh, don't you feel silly.)

How is that our little human minds can hold all this knowledge and yet be so ignorant that we forget to lift the most important thing of all: God. God is high and lifted and it is important that we put him in the right perspective. People who worship other God's and things are often in prayer and devotion to those things. We must prioritize God above everything and put Him first and give him our best. I have found that there have been many times in my life when I was out of order. I had God included in the program of my life but just not first and I struggled because of this. With my own human might I tried to make things happen and suffered unnecessarily because of my decision on this.

As you grow in your Christian faith, you learn to prioritize. It's like making a list of daily things to do and adding God up top. Okay, here is a sample. I would wake up and go wash, drink my coffee, and eat my breakfast. Kiss my kids and husband and on the way to drop them off say a quick prayer for God's protection. Then I began to grow and as I did my routine changed. I would wake up then get washed and dressed. Pray over my breakfast then kiss my family. I'd pray in the car as I dropped them off and then pray before going to work. In a little time, I grew a little more I'd wake up and pray, get washed and dressed. Pray over my breakfast then kiss my kids and pray before going to work and ask for protection even for us all day and on the way home. Now I pray, I fast, and I watch sermons for inspiration on repeat meditation on the word given in an attempt to learn more about God and my help. I still wake up and pray and might I add my hubby prays with me though not as much yet for him. I do all the other things above and add in praying at night and sometimes waking up one to two hours before everyone to have alone time with God.

Today, I value spending time alone with God. I know the importance of spending time to remember Him and to prioritize God in my life. My parents taught me to reverence the house of God (church) and to keep it holy and that I will do. I may be a little ratchet at times, but I will not disrespect the House of God. It makes me think of the story in the Bible where King David and his peeps were bringing the Ark of the Covenant back from the Philistines. Well one homie, Uzziah, noticed the ark was tipping, and he attempted to reach out and uphold it. Bad move because the ark's center was a container that housed the "glory of God." When this dude touched the ark, he dropped dead. This isn't the best part yet keep reading a little further.

When King David and the boys observed this, they were able to secure the ark of God, but they learned a fast lesson. They moved forward walking with the ark but every so many steps would take a break and pause and put it down. When they did, they took a minute to give God glory and therefore, they remembered Him! What this teaches my full-grown self is to put proper things in perspective. It teaches me that I am a human, but God is Our Father, and he needs no assistance from humans to be who He is. Brother Uzziah, I am sorry for your loss, sir. You took one for the team and I hope when you got to glory, they gave you a good spot by a pretty tree or fancy river.

Today I am incredibly careful to keep God in his rightful place on the throne and without comparison. I also see God in and throughout creation and it helps me to remember him. When I see a rainbow after the sunshine it helps me to remember God. I also get the reminder of God when I see a beautiful scenery in colors it makes me remember that Dad is an artist. My best reminder of all is watching a beautiful sunset off the horizon of a pretty clear blue beach. I love and observe the way that the beach has its boundaries and so does the ocean. The sky has a boundary as it meets the water, and it reminds me of how God separated the firmaments in the beginning, and it is good!

Another thing to remember is we have a set time here on Earth for each of us. No one knows how long they will be here, and some never make it. Each person serves a purpose and God has a specific plan for their life. Some are sent here to only be babies, other children some adults, and other seniors. While we are gifted these years to live, we must remember to pay thanks to the giver. Don't waste your life living here like this is only all about yourself. If you do, you will have fooled yourself. It is said that all of creation gives praise in their own way to God. Now let me tell you I don't want to walk past screaming trees or yelling grass. Just do your due diligence and so will I and remember to remember the Creator.

CHAPTER 23

A COVERING FOR MY HEAD

As a female we are taught that our hair is symbolic of our beauty. Though hair is simply a covering for your head. Mostly everyone has hair except for some people who have health conditions, a few babies, and those who choose to be bald. Hair is a protective coating or covering for our delicate areas like our brains, our underarms, and even our genitals. A covering is something that keeps us from being exposed and is like a shield.

Now this thought may be out of context, but I am reminded of it as I sit here under a hairdryer in my favorite hairdresser's salon. Since hair is a physical covering, then it may as well be spectacular. It should be lustrous and healthy, also shiny and elegant. Just think of the last time when you saw someone with fabulous hair, what did you think? I will tell you; you said look at his/her hair it is gorgeous. (That's right, that is exactly what you said.)

When I am not at the salon, I have a job to maintain my tresses on my own at home. It is my task to keep it neat and beautiful. Some of my favorite supplies include shampoo, conditioner, essential oils, scalp brushes, combs, hairbrushes, and finally the bonnet. A bonnet is a covering women often use on their heads at night to protect their hairstyles. Some variations of this include using a headscarf or even a silk or satin pillowcase. Wearing these head coverings keep African American hair from breakage and often from drying out at night, protecting the hairstyles from damage.

A big thank you is due to one of my favorite stars of today, Mrs. Tabitha Brown. Ro (hubby) and I follow her podcast and we caught an episode that she and her husband did, and it talked about hair bonnets. The episode wasn't solely focused on this, but I modeled a little piece of this in our relationship to keep things fun and playful. I enjoyed watching this podcast, but my husband wasn't so happy when he decided to sit in at the table and hear what was being said. Let's just say he has a new love-hate relationship for hair bonnets now!

My husband loves when my hair looks like I just came from the salon. He loves to see women in short hair but I food out he fantasizes about when I have different looks via wigs (Honey, that is another story and for that we may need a second book.) Mrs. Brown explained that her end-of-night routine involved her bonnet being placed on which meant that was the close of initiating any sexual or heavy intimate relations. Then I was a copycat and after my skincare bedtime regiment started to implement pulling out my night cap and boy, he snapped. I laughed so hard for about a week at this man. He threatened me that he didn't care what I heard but that he wasn't going to let a haircap stop him from doing anything. My guy told me he would toss my bonnet out the window and I couldn't help laughing until my belly hurt.

On another level I look at it like he didn't want me to cover my head because he feels that he is my covering. (I may be reaching but you're smart.) My husband is in many ways my covering. He guides this family and protects us by making decisions he knows will keep us all safe. He is a safe place to confide in when I have trouble or distress. When I am weak in strength or sick, broke, or discouraged, he willfully gives these things to me. My husband is a great covering and in so many ways he reminds me of my father. That is my earthly father who is no longer here and my heavenly Father who is always here. (I said in many ways he is my covering.) God is our covering and his reach is greater than ours.

Then who is his covering? Survey says, God! God is the head of our household just as my husband is the head of this house. Sis this isn't easy to say and not because I am prideful but because I was taught to be a strong Black woman who didn't need anyone to complete her. Well, I learned that I am not always that strong, also it is ok to need help and why not get it from a good spouse? At times I get disheartened because he does not yet have a big relationship with God. Hubby knows of God and was even taught of him as a child, but he had a tough childhood.

He grew up going to Catholic school and even told me at one time he was an altar server. Ro was in the choir even until sports became a bigger part of his life. Why then would I be disheartened because I felt he didn't get the chance to develop his relationship with God in his youth. His mom passed away when he was a boy of only eight years old. Being a mom, myself, makes me feel no one will nurture you like your mom. Often mothers share their spiritual faith with their children. Without having his mom here to nurture that bond I felt it didn't grow because he didn't have such a connection. He was blessed to have two wonderful stepmoms. (One at a time people.) Many lovely ladies in his community gave him love, fed him, and taught him skills a mother would.

I think by marrying me I have been a considerable influence on his life due to my intentional walk with God. That's right, you heard me. I may have used to fight and cuss but I am never giving up my relationship with God. My man's faith is growing in God, and I am so happy for him. Yes, I love my husband and want to see him develop and walk with God, daily and totally. Today he is growing and worships God with me even singing praise music with me. In the last five years his faith has increased dramatically. Although from time to time I may have to tell him we shouldn't cuss people out even when we know they deserve it, pray for us! My bae is still a work in progress but aren't we all? Yes. Not one of us in this world is perfect.

Just a few years ago a man that never prayed out loud today prays out loud once a week and even attends church quarterly with some convincing. We pray together early every Sunday morning as I share my faith with him and tell him how when two touch and agree God stands in the midst. Yes, I had to re-direct him from praying for being rich, asking for cars, or asking God to add additional length to his boy toy!

Remember, this is still a book with humor; keep it light, fam! Hubby prays that God helps us pay off all our debt, blesses us to bless others so we can donate what we have to help others, and to have meaningful intimacy which is more important that the first half of his prayer.

We all must start somewhere on our own faith journey. His journey is not mine and vice versa. I was born into a family that participated in church, worship, and teaching about God as a baby. No matter where you are on the steps to glory the most important thing is to just be on the steps. I picture our depths of being in God are like climbing the stairway to Heaven. Think about playing a video game that is good and trying to make your way up to the next level. Imagine being Mario jumping your way up the blocks escaping danger on your way to save the princess. We all start out on step one which is like being on a flat stone, something like being at the bat at home base. As we grow in depth of knowing God, we advance but up a stairwell to the next level. Some of you may not comprehend this but I know I got all of you gamers to follow! Every step we take we elevate and advance to a new level. Each new level, you guessed it, comes with a "new devil" or a set of trials, set back, temptations or danger meant to throw us off. This is when we get to experience our Lord's covering for us, over us. It keeps us protected and endows us with what we need to move through the next level and move up the next step.

To make it plain, God is my covering just like my bonnet is my covering for my hair. Although, He does things on such more of a grandiose level that my tiny little human heart can't even fathom. Trust me, no matter how much I spend on a headscarf or bonnet it will never be as secure. It could be silk or satin, it could be stretchy, and none of this even matters. Abba (Father) is the ultimate covering, and he is vast enough to cover every one of us in this world. My friends if you need someone bigger, greater, and mightier than you, God is.

Let's put his ability to cover into proper perspective. In the beginning God created and I am paraphrasing but the Earth was formless, empty, and dark, and the spirit of God was hovering over the waters. He was hovering over the entire waters of all the world. So how big exactly is that? Immeasurable. You try to hover over all the world and then tell me how you were able to stretch yourself enough to compensate for it and I will wait. Should you come for me to tell me this, so you know in advance I am going to call you a liar. Don't come to me with all this craziness because I know better than this. I may not be a molecular doctor of quantum physics or what have you, but my science brain tells me this is humanly impossible.

What is impossible to humans is possible with God. It is a great feeling to rest under the covering of God. It is like a baby being nestled under the covering of a warm blanket, loved and safe. If you need protection in this world, if you need to feel safe and be covered, come to God. As much as I joke around in this, I am dead serious when I say that no one can be for you who God is. Not a spouse, a parent, or a best friend can be as loving and protecting as He is. Finally, I relent in saying a bonnet holds no weight to God when it comes to covering. In this case you may as well pull it off. To my hubby I know that you are waiting to troll, aka "read" this book, taking off my bonnet is not a co-sign for you, sir!

CHAPTER 24

WHAT DO YOU NEED RESURRECTED?

It is Lent season which is the period of forty days before Easter. During this time Christians remember the sacrifice Jesus gave by giving up his life for us. In remembrance we often decide on something to give up for a period of forty days that lead up to Easter. The good news is that Jesus got up from the dead. He is our resurrected savior! What does this even mean in plain language? Glad you asked, I will explain it. As we go living from day to day with time some of the things we have or do can quickly become out of date. This can include things like our slang, clothing, even our hairstyles and yes, our shoe game. At some point we stop and take inventory of these things and notice that these things need being revamped, replaced, refreshed. This is in some ways a form of a resurrection, which is the coming back to life after death. I said it and your sense of style may be dead and in need of resurrection and that's okay, love. I went through a phase like this about seven years ago. Yes, even I go through this. My marriage was going well but things seemed a little mundane. Just so you are aware your girl likes options and keeps things interesting. I started to change my hairstyles and to add unique style clothing to my wardrobe and I find that this helps me to stay edgy. You do not have to be rich to do this. Start by adding a few new things, accessories, a new haircut, or a few flashy pairs of sunglasses. Boo, just do you. Most importantly don't let anyone make you forget who you are and to be your authentic self. Your personal clothing or sense of fashion style is just one type of resurrection we need from time to time.

Much more importantly than that is you. If you have not accepted Christ as your savior by confession and belief, then you are as dated as your old style. Then, my friend, you also need a resurrection. If you do already know him great but sometimes even, we can re-dedicate our lives to him. Now let's look at how it is that we end up needing this to happen in our lives. On a physical level it's easy to accept that we age, and our clothes get dated. Our sense of style or music can get dated and even how we relate with the culture can be dated because each generation brings innovative ideas and a new style. Let's look at the culture and see how this is true. Our grandparents rocked hot pressed hair comb styles and some of the men had lye presses in their hair. Moving on, we moved to high top fades for the brothers and the sisters dubbed those French rolls, mushrooms, and pin curled looks. Don't get it twisted, it's now summer of 2024 and I heard those French rolls are coming back, but I don't want them! Later came along the fade for our men and relaxers for our women with wraps and even short hair styles. Today some are rocking natural hair, and the guys are even going back to high top hair with side fades with what's known as the spongy look up top. Others like me also are donning the short pixie haircuts, hey.

Whatever, all of this is fleeting because, as we see, things change every generation. Then what else in our lives can die and need to be resurrected? Our love lives or dreams or even our faith needs a resurrection. They say it is better to have "loved and lost then never to have loved at all." I say while there may be some truth to that it is still good when you are alone to have a resurrection in your love life and meet and have someone new to love again with. Love is one of the greatest feelings in the world and it is essential for our growth, and I believe aids in our longevity. Don't believe me? Here is an example, then. We all know the old couple who have been married over fifty to seventy years or more and are going on together until they die. Love makes you fight differently even when you feel like giving up on yourself.

Loving someone else so deeply makes you want to endure all things for them. This is how God loves us, and Jesus' resurrection was a demonstration of what perfect, unfailing love looks like. Who has ever had a dream that over time has gotten lost? I have. Look at a child next time you're in their presence and observe how they are such great creatives. Children can dream so big and as we grow into adults, we begin to put limits on ourselves. Sometimes, adults are fearful to reach for their dreams or put dreams on hold for the sake of their families or finances or some other reason. Today, I am your witness that you can live out your dreams. Pull them back out of your drawer or your secret place and ask God for a resurrection.

I have been creative since I was a young child. I loved to dream, draw, dance, and do all things that involved color art and creativity. As a young adult I was scared to attempt to live these dreams out because people told me I could not. I was told by teachers and by boyfriends that I could not achieve things I proposed to do and accomplish. They were all wrong. I can and will do all that I dream, and I ask the good Master to give me bigger dreams in 2024! This is the year that my dreams are being resurrected and completed and this could be your year as well.

Ask God to resurrect your dreams and if you're not sure how, here is a template. God, I know your busy. I thank you for being bigger than anything in life. I pray you will always cover for me and forgive me my sins. Lord, please resurrect my dreams. Make them bigger than I ever expected and help me to accomplish them. Help me not to shrink but to grow tall and strong like you want me to be. While doing this for me create new dreams for me to discover I have. Thank you for a moment in time. Your thankful servant (place your name here). Amen. See, that was easier than you thought it would be.

We covered our sense of style, our need for love in our lives and our dreams. Who, though, needs their faith to be resurrected? I have been there too. I now have both my parents who have gone on to leave this world and we spoke on that. I spoke a little about being depressed after my mom died. What I didn't share was for a short while and I am embarrassed, but somehow, I seemed to have lost my faith. I was in a dark place and let me tell you I am not a dark person by nature. When she died, I swore off drawing and art and threw away many of my sketch books of work I had done over the years. That wasn't the darkest part though. The darkest part was how I avoided going to church for at least a few months because I felt God could have changed the circumstances and he did not. I was angry at God, and I thought I could turn my back for a moment to make it right. I was wrong but I feel that a lot of people may be going through or gone through less and feel or felt the same.

Today, I know that loving God and being faithful is not predicated on my feelings. Feelings are not a good indicator of Spirit. They are unstable and ever changing daily and sometimes from moment to moment. I will share at this time how I got back my faith. I had someone share some words of encouragement to give me. They told me how my mother loved me and how she would want me to go on. My mother was a Christian, and she praised at my dad's funeral, and I couldn't understand why at that time. Now, she wasn't laughing out loud or anything, but she was thanking God, worshipping at his casket, and I couldn't comprehend it. I believe my mother was seeking God to ask for encouragement to go on. She was having her faith resurrected while we were having a funeral service. The Bible says how faith comes by hearing the word of God. I have been hearing this word since I was a young girl. Then that meant that faith was inside of me even when I was grieving. If you are out there and you are grieving, you can have a resurrection of your faith. If you do not know the word of God, you can open the Bible and began to read, meditate, and repeat the words of the book. I hope to pour out my heart to those who are suffering, those in anguish who are utterly heartbroken as I was when I lost my mother. My mother was agi when I was a teenager which is a new age term for aggravation. In my adult life, though, she called me on the phone every day and checked in on my family, my children, me. I haven't had another friend yet who has done such as my mom. What I have had is the ability to go to God and talk to him every day like I did with my mom. I know he listens to me and responds although not in the same way. God is a mother to the motherless and a father to the fatherless.

In all that I have said to you I want you to know that you deserve your resurrection. Not just a resurrection in faith alone either but a total resurrection you deserve. A quickening (an old word you don't hear much), an awakening of your mind, body and soul. Every good and perfect gift comes from God, and he has so much to give to you. The church I go to now is a non-denominational Christian church, but I love that they preach on abundance. They teach on how God is a good God, how he loves you and he wants to bless you. This year June will be my first year of attendance at this church.

Prior to that I attended a Methodist church from 2006-2023. I departed after the church had a lot of conflict over some issues. Prior to that, from birth to 1995, I was a member of a Baptist church like all my family. Regardless, I love God and believe Christ died for me. He was raised from the dead and wants the best and expects the best of me and this is what I am walking in today. Friends, I have already experienced one resurrection, this one of my faith, but when you see me in the streets, shout me out and tell me what you have been resurrected from.

CHAPTER 25

HOW CAN YOU KISS IT?

A cross today is a well-known symbol. Most people recognize it to identify someone who practices the Christian faith. People wear their necklaces on shirts and clothing and even tattoo it on their skin. Often, we make the things of God too casual. We try to reduce the things of God that are vast down to a scale we can relate with. Despite showing people what we want them to believe about our faith we are better off demonstrating how we live it out for them.

The cross in many ways was thought to be a curse. It was a shameful and harsh form of execution for criminals. The Bible spoke of how cursed everyone was who was hung on a tree. Tattoos are artwork that are inked into the skin to be permanent. Necklaces are usually made of some type of metal like gold and silver. Crosses were constructed of wood made from trees, usually cedar, pine, and cypress. Two pieces of wood were assembled perpendicular to form the shape of a cross. After that they were mounted into the ground and a prisoner would be nailed to it then hung until they bled out and died. It was a type of capital punishment much like we now have electric chairs, gas, and death from lethal injections. Regardless, it is death, and it is final.

What is good is that because we are born in sin, we all deserve the death sentence. However, God is merciful and just. He sent Jesus his only son embodied in flesh. Being both God and man he went to the cross, blameless with no sin, and died for us as our substitution. Jesus was perfect and his death by sacrifice broke the hold sin had on man. It opened a door for us to get back in fellowship with God. God now can see us through the lens of Christ and have a relationship with us. Jesus embodied in flesh while being both God and man, went to the cross and died as our substitution. Being God he was perfect and blameless and without any sin.

Christ's death by sacrifice broke the hold of sin off man by opening a door for us to get back in fellowship with God by way of choice via our own free wills. Yes, that's what I said, God gave us the ability to choose to be in relationship with him. He did not force us or make us like robots but gave man free will. For three days Jesus remained in the grave, but he came out resurrected to life and is all powerful and victorious. Jesus took the keys of hell, death, and the grave and he has total power over all of these and everything.

Here is a Lynette translation for all of you. Jesus', aka Emmanuel God, chose us even over himself. As we live this life, at some point, we do have hard days, but how many of us can say they had a good Friday that ended in their own death? Today for some of us Friday's is one of our favorite days of the week. It is one of my favorite days. Imagine being in Jesus' shoes and knowing death was coming for you that day. He asked the homies, his closest, to come with him and to go pray with him. Meanwhile, they are over in the corner nodding off at a most serious time for their Lord. It makes you realize that even with good friends you may sometime have to go through your own hard deal on your own. Just because you are surrounded by people, it doesn't necessarily mean you still can't be alone.

Next Jesus endured verbal attacks of his character and torture while being dragged back and forth between two governors. Finally, it was decided he should be put into the hands of His people to decide his judgement. The same people who he healed and blessed, taught, and fed together decided they would issue him a death sentence. I mean, they had no remorse, people. Doesn't this sound like the people of today? You could be in association and be eating and hanging out and living life together and in a moment, they could turn around and speak your downfall.

Now when I insert myself in this plot, had I been in the position that Jesus was I would want to say you ungrateful mother-children… I caught myself friends. From here he is taunted and tortured even more until he is finally hung up after being nailed to a wooden cross and left to die. Let's now talk about that cross that he bore. Imagine being beaten like a punching bag then given a heavy wooden cross to carry yourself to use for your own death. (No, sir, I wish I would.) He was paired with a man from some portion of his distance to the cross to help him carry the cross. Then at the intended point he was nailed hands and feet spiked to the cross and raised up to his end.

How foretelling it is that he was born into a family that by trade were known to be carpenters. A carpenter works with creating and reshaping wood structures. With the thing he worked with and crafted for others that very same thing was used as an instrument in his own death. Then I had to take a step back and take a panoramic look at this. The cross was the means our savior gave himself for us to be able to get to God. Some call it a curse but for me it is a cure.

Jesus being crucified and lifted was the cure for sin and was for all of humanity. A scripture in the Bible states how if he be lifted from the Earth he would draw all men to him. I am blessed in this now and have access to God. Satan made a mistake. He meant to kill the son of God and by doing so leaving man without a chance to get back to God. This would have left all of us in hell after death without a chance to fulfill the sin requirement. Jesus Christ's sacrifice would save all humans who accept and believe in him.

Don't ask me then how it is I can kiss my cross; how can I not? Jesus's sacrifice on the cross was my saving grace. (I feel one of the church aunties right here coming out and singing, Amazing Grace.) I will take up and carry my own cross because that is my Christian duty. It is the least that I can do in my service. If Christ could dutifully carry the weight of the sins of all in the world to death, then I can do my part which in comparison is miniscule. Do I like to undergo hardships and face adversity? What do you think?

Adversity and trials can be due to demonic forces at work. Hardship and troubles may also be commissioned by God to grow us, teach us ,or grab our attention. Regardless of this my duty is to live and do my part in carrying my cross. I will walk on with my burdens and my blessings and my hardships. This may be my lot, but this is how I am able to kiss it. Why? Because I could never do what Christ has done for me. Christ is perfect and I am not. I am human and love him but am sinful, petty, corruptible, manipulative. These are words I feel I can choke on, but we must honestly see ourselves. This doesn't mean I do not try to be like Jesus. I do, I really, really do most of the time (see how that works).

The sight of the cross helps me put things into perspective. It keeps me accountable for my actions, thoughts, and my being. When I see it being elevated, it reminds me that I too must be elevated. I can't be like this world and its people because God set me apart. The price he paid was great and unparallel. Many times, while I am living this human existence, I come up short of how I should be practicing and living my walk with God. Note to reader: We are all human and from time to time we do come up short. When my flesh wants to be arrogant, cocky, lazy, feisty, or distant, I can't succumb to these feelings. I cannot let Lynette on the outside win against me. Spirit Nette-Nette (my childhood nickname) is soft and gentle, kind, and has self-control. More importantly, she makes me be patient, strategic, faithful, and powerful.

The cross was a gateway for Jesus to defeat sin and resurrect to God in Heaven with all power. My cross is also a gateway and a portal for me to complete my assignment God created me for and when the vessel is empty return to him. It's much like some of these new age animes where I am the vessel, and my gifts are my Jujitsu which I am amplified through fashion and art like I am in my God borne domain. Okay, I may be watching too much anime. These Millennial's and Gen Z will get what I am trying to say. Go ask your kids or your nieces and nephews what I am talking about. Once my vessel's (body) spirit is emptied out and completed its purpose it will shed the flesh and return to God. Now, so we are clear I am in no rush for this to take place anytime soon. I have too much work and living to do right now!

I am working daily, quarterly, even annually on myself and becoming better. Then I am asking God to work on my family and their salvation and then their growth and multiplication. My work will be to spread the goodness and love of God to people in the world and to do it by giving them a smile. By sharing some light and bringing some laughter you can bring joy and healing to a lot of people. Sharing God and salvation to people is equally important to bring souls to Christ. I plan to expand to the different avenues of media including my favorites—the fashion, art, and comedy—and to the edgy car lovers all over the world and to all we encounter there is forgiveness and hope and redemption in God. Don't just look up and see a cross. Get up and go up. See the Christ who conquered it and did everything unimaginable he could to have a relationship with you, and for you to have a relationship with God. How can you not kiss it? The cross is both our burden and our freedom.

CHAPTER 26

RAINBOWS WITHOUT RAIN

I don't know if you are aware of this friend, but we can have rainbows without rain. For me, this is like a fresh new breath of air. To understand this more, we need to first examine both above. A rainbow is an arch of visible colors seen resulting from the reflection or refraction of water droplets. While rain is moisture accumulated in the clouds that then get dropped to the ground once the clouds are over saturated and no longer able to contain the water.

Then how is it that one can exist without the other? Simple, one can stand alone. Bookmark this thought and we will circle back around to it. Rainbows can exist even without rain. They can reflect other forms of water like mist, sprays, and even dew. Therefore, it is not necessary to have rain for you to see a rainbow. To me something about this just sounds wrong.

What could be more perfect than a beautiful display of colors after the rain has stopped? Rainbows are colorful and are often associated with luck and with religion and in today's day also represent a symbol that stands for gender inclusion. I am always happy when I see a rainbow in the sky. Not long ago on a particular rainy day I was even able to see two in the same area in one day. Rainbows are simply one of the world's most brilliant phenomena. After some self-reflection I wonder why it is most people think of a rainbow being pleasant and they think on the rain being displeasing. The rain is a necessary component of our weather system. Rain is nurturing in that it provides water and it exists in a renewable cycle. Our animals, plants, trees, and us all need the rain.

Without water humans and many of the breathing, living things on this Earth cannot exist.

Rain is in several ways a cleanser. It pours down from the upper atmosphere to offer hydration to many things. Have you ever in your childhood went outside during the rain and opened your mouth to try to catch raindrops in your mouth? Or you were one of the kids that would cup your hands together and try to catch enough drops to drink. How about the animals? They don't use cups unless they are domesticated. Don't they put their mouths to the ground and drink the collected water drops to clench their thirst? Didn't God once in history past send the Great Flood to cleanse the Earth and rid the world of all humans except Noah and his family? That, my friends, felt cleansing.

My husband has a conspiracy theory that being wet on the head by rainwater makes you sick. He tells me that he believes there is something in the rain that does this. Perhaps. What if rainwater does the opposite of this? Think of the animals and how happy and content they are when they play in the rain. The ducks and birds, otters, badgers, and mosquitos all of them and they are rain crazy. Maybe when the rain hits our head, it sorts of cleanses us of impurities, like the water of Baptism. Humanity in the beginning was pure when we existed in the garden with God. Sin came into the world by the trickery of Satan and changed our essence and our original forms. In our living we must make the choice and intention to repent and be baptized then get back to God. No, forty-minute showers are not going to do it.

When I think of water purifying it also reminds me of waterfalls. They are refreshing and cleansing, and not only do they look beautiful, but they give us a sense of joy. Rain is also like a form of therapy. Many of today's applications use the sound of rain or pictures of it as meditation. When it rains, I like to sit at home and stare out of my window looking at it fall. Don't get me wrong, I respect Jesus so if I see lightning, I'm leaving the window! In many ways the sound of rain helps me to relax. There is no way I am the only human out here who likes to fall asleep at the sound of the heavy rain falling. I mean I even must catch myself from falling asleep when I get my hair washed much like a baby. Best of all I like to look at the rain falling during the night. There is something about the contrast of a dark sky and the droplets falling that fascinates me.

Why does the rain then get a negative rap? Rain at times can put a damper on our plans, especially certain outdoor events. I've heard people say too many days of rain coming makes them feel depressed. There is even childhood song like rain, rain go away. Hold tight to your pants or panties as I share this next one with you. I was told when it rained it was because "the devil was beating his wife." Huh? I know that some of these folk tales of the past need to die. Don't you sit there and think I am about to try and explain that one. Not!

My realization is that we need the rain. Rain falling during a wedding is also thought to bring luck. I don't believe in luck, but I do believe in a long life. Just like we need the sunshine and rainbows we also need rain. We need balance in this life. Day and night ,up and down, in and out, yin and yang. Life Is all about balance, relationships, and perspective. There are times when we can change our perspective on things and see what we once thought bad as good. Take the rainbow and the rain too.

CHAPTER 27

THIS FLESH AIN'T IT

What is it then about this flesh of ours? It is like our outer protective clothing, much like the animals have fur or exoskeletons or skin. The funny thing about it is not always as protective as it should be. Flesh tears and wrinkles, it scars, and truthfully to some degree it is somewhat vulnerable. Don't forget its layers can shed and after some time left stagnant, it can decay. Without having an inner core, it has no life and just lays out like meat.

Why do we even have it? I am not God don't ask me! Just joking. I imagine its purpose is to give us a sort of outer defense for our body. The Bible says how we (humans)were made in the image of God and in his likeness. To first understand this clearly you must be aware that God is not flesh He is spirit. Our inner being is also made of Spirit and it is that which was made in the image of God, I think. Then why is it that some people are or choose to be evil on the inside? Easy, it is the free will of choice. Remember though as a child born into this world God deposited a spirit inside each baby that lives.

In our beginning, God took our flesh-born bodies and inserted a spirit man inside him. That reference is not gender specific. This spirit lives encased inside of a soul that contains our thoughts, emotions, and our personality. Finally, this soul lives inside the body which is our flesh. In many ways this reminds me of a good thing like some caramel filled chocolates. Or like the pleasant experience of biting into an ice cream cone that has a different flavor of filling on the inside. Having a spirit inside of me makes me capable of being in the likeness of my Father.

This is a gift given by God to humans only and for it we are favored. Why do I think this? Because God sent Christ to reconcile the relationship with us. It was a sacrifice for humans, not for animals, not for angels, but for all of us! This may have been wordy but a point I wanted to make here is sometimes things can be better on the inside than on the outside. People spend so much money on plastic surgery and crazy diets and all these skincare regiments to doll up and perfect the body and their souls are lost.

I can remember lollipops in my childhood that had candy or gum in the center, and they were delicious, right? Or imagine the prettiest gift-wrapping paper when you open it without thought gets thrown to the ground once you find a better, worthier gift inside. In this same way the spirit that lives in us is just as precious. When we accept God as our personal savior it becomes saved. Then it is the job of our spirit, our control center, to work out our life plan of subjecting itself and the body to following the Spirit of God and not the world.

This makes a thinker like me wonder for just a moment why then wasn't the spirit on the outside and the flesh on the inside of us. In a human's case I think it was because our flesh is corruptible. We inherit sin as soon as we are born into this world due to the curse of the garden.

God is omniscient meaning all-knowing, He never wanted us to know sin. Not in our body, souls, or spirit, I believe. God is many things just so you do not get confused reading this. He says in the Word that his name is I AM that I AM which means He is all things. God is a consuming fire and many ways he is a refiner. He can simply rid the outer containment and leave the purest form which is like pure gold. I believe this is the meaning of our lives, to have the choice to accept God or not and be refined during the process to salvation or decide on your eternal death. That's your business. We go through the mapped-out plan of God for our days and at the end the flesh is destroyed leaving solely the spirit. Hopefully, you at this point have made a good decision to choose God for your life. I can tell you that this is my plan. I do not plan to die and eternally burn in hell and be tortured, no thanks. While

I am on this path, I also have a lot of time I can spend to develop and grow my spirit, my faith, and my love.

I can hear some of you out there saying how you will not let nobody burn you. Okay, go ahead and execute a will that says you do not want to be cremated as your choice. You wouldn't want your body to saved only to experience your spirit being burned. No matter if you are buried in a casket or cremated, we all one day will leave this Earth and not by our own will. The unique thing that makes you yourself by this time in your journey will have parted. I'm sorry, but I had to break it to you like that.

Many people invest so much of their time, money and effort on the development and alteration of their outer appearance. Most are non-believers who feel they are here to live their best life. There exist many people who believe that their body is a temple. I do although I am not a 100 percent health fanatic. In keeping this temple, we need to eat well and exercise, get good sleep and remain active. This is a needed formula for long physical endurance of the body. However, this does not do anything for the development of your spirit man. For my life I am a firm believer of balance. Call it an epiphany if you need it but your spirit must first be awakened. We must realize God exists and decide to choose him of our own free will. Faith comes by hearing and this hearing comes from the word of God. These words were written and recorded in the bible. When Jesus was alive, there was no Bible at that time. It was a compilation of works of faith people walking with God prior to Jesus being born. It is also followers capturing his works and living and provision for people after he left. In the same way that we invest in treating and developing our bodies we should do the same with our spirits. We must devote time to spend with God daily. We learn by studying the Bible, meditating on the words, and learning the heart of God. Our energy needs to be expelled to chase after the things of God. We need to use our money to invest in building the kingdom of God here on Earth by sponsoring things that support this movement. We need to buy and read things that are Christian related like books, games and even merchandise.

We must search for God with the same tenacity we do for the things of this world. I say go looking for God like you would a designer bag that is on sale for a little money. Look for God like you would your favorite perfume in a department store that is about to be discontinued. Search for God like we search for them perfect outfits to wear out to try and impress people. Don't judge me, but after reading the above you can clearly see my thought process. Abba (Father) must become your number one priority. Daily and intentionally make time and space to spend with God. One of my favorite places to seek God is in my entryway of my home early in the morning before anyone wakes up. I am talking three or four in the morning. One thing I love to do is to write in my journal to God.

My first entry to God started by me writing a handwritten letter to him when I was about twenty-three years old and sticking it into a shoebox in my closet. I should have had an idea that I would one day author books because I am creative and most definitely have an opinion. It has not always been this way for me since as a child I often felt ignored and silenced. I was one in my family of four children, three adults, and grandchildren. I was the youngest female in my family then of five women so everyone older than me felt my opinion was the least needed. Then as an adolescent and young adult I was often overlooked because I was young and Black American. Not just this but we also grew up in an era being instructed children were to be seen and not heard. I do not totally agree with this though I believe children should have a place and know it. I also believe it is important to let your children speak to express themselves and their thoughts to you.

Today I have decided to use my upbringing to my advantage. I am not often the first to speak because I have learned patience. I like to wait, and this often leads others around me to question me on what is my stance? It is then at that time that I weigh in and after some thought respond when most impactful.

I started my prayer journal box and wasn't committed to it at first. I heard a sermon in church in NY about praying in secret in my closet and God blessing me openly. I took this literally, and I prayed in my closet and at times deposited a new letter for God to read in that shoe box. Then I got married and moved from the state and had no clue what my mom did with that shoe box as I moved away from my childhood home. I decided at that point to make it an annual letter to God. I moved twice since my childhood home so I couldn't keep up any longer with a shoebox. That does not mean that I forgot to write the letters to God. I would write in the letter how grateful I was to him for his blessings. If I was troubled by any current situation, I would ask him to send a solution in the letter. Then I would end my letter to Him by reminding him that I was still his daughter and close with a thank you. I forgot to share with you that in some of these letters I would also vent to Him.

The year 2023 was remarkably busy for me. It was the first year of me catching up with many things since 2020. I know we were all affected by 2020 and so many of our lives were shaken and turned upside down. It felt in many ways like I was still catching up with things from three years prior and still was running behind. I don't think I had a chance to write my annual letter to Daddy since. Yes, I do call him daddy since my biological father is in heaven with him today.

I have no doubt that God reads my letters! God is omniscient remember, so you may thing I am wasting time. He knows the thoughts I have before I can even write them down. Though for some reason I have always felt I can express myself better in words than verbally. He sits on his throne in his holy temple and laughs at me like "little human Lynette" he sits and says out loud she needed to express that so she can heal and move forward. One year later and I can say that today I am more comfortable verbally expressing to him what I need to say in prayer and talks.

Regardless, it is fine for me, and he knows I like to write. Today, I don't find it ironic that I am now on my way as an Indie author. Now I may not have the best penmanship but in my younger years I have often felt stronger in writing my feelings down on paper. Writing allowed me to have a voice when everything in my childhood told me to be seen and not heard. God is all knowing, and he is omnipresent. God is in all places at the same time, everywhere. I never have to wait for God to arrive somewhere. He has all knowledge, so he never is blindsided like us or puzzled; nothing surprises God. More importantly He is all powerful and nothing is to strong or great for him to handle. Which means to me he could read what I write and do nothing. He also could decide to read and do something to change my situation. God is Elohim (Creator) and one thing about this is He could always create something new. Our past experiences and our skill sets are both used in the assignments he has for our lives. I heard a pastor say God never wastes anything, I wish I could remember who they were,

What this leaves me with in the end is a new perspective. I will try to do good and be good and sometimes this flesh will fail. I have God who is mightier than me in all his ways. He can see all, do all is all powerful and can be everywhere at once. It makes me rest in the fact that I have a full-proof plan and it is to trust in God. Writing words on paper made me feel like I could get something personal to the attention of God. I can do this without paper. God is waiting to hear from me and you. He welcomes your prayers, and you can get to him through prayer. God did say in the Bible that vengeance is his. Now if you decide to write a ratchet letter to God about someone's nonsense to free you, then do it! Just don't forget, we have made mistakes, and we too are ratchet or have been at some point in our lives. Once you have cleared your head, then ask for repentance. Yes, I said it. God requires us to be holy and to pull down thoughts that don't line up with how he wants us to live. I believe in you and yes you can do this. It is just like those nights we all sneak up for a late-night snack and eat one too many cookies or too big of a slice of leftover meatloaf or have that second glass of wine. Here is where I clear my throat friends, we said we would minimize or eliminate the wine. The homie Paul in the Bible said it best, that even when he wants to do good evil is always present with me. We must come to learn and realize this flesh we have fails us. Thankfully, we have a helper God that can help us to always overcome. Simply put, this rebellious flesh gets on my nerves! That is why we need the Holy Spirit inside of us.

CHAPTER 28

HAIR SHOP GOSSIP AND BARBER BLUFFS

Black hair care is important! It is much more than a simple boost of self-esteem. It is a way we socialize, laugh together, and pass on important info in the community. It is networking at its finest in our culture. For many of us these shops are considered safe spaces. Over the years the generations of Black people in America have acquired a deep-felt love for these services and the people who inhabit them. We have come to know them as places of comfort. Places where it is ok to let down our guards and be our genuine selves.

How could you not be vulnerable when you are out in public to get your hair serviced? I believe that slavery did something to our race to strip us of being confident. We hide our hair when it is messy, at least I know I do at times. I am certain if we were back in our native country, we would be strong, proud, unyielding, and not held hostage to our hair. Trust me, I am proud of us who have already begun to do this by going natural or letting our hair grow out or in locs. My daughter and nieces have gone natural and even my son refuses to get a haircut but don a high-top fade hairstyle with his natural tight curly hair longer and higher than mine. I absolutely love that for us. I, myself though, feel better with some product in this head. I have, however, vowed that by fifty in just a few years I am going to make a change.

For most of us, getting our hair serviced by a salon or barber helps us to get our hair clean and manageable. It is here that we can bounce off ideas on each other and share both like and un-alike opinions. My husband has helped me decode the insides of a barbershop. I have been in barbershops back in NY and in Virginia and I know it goes down at the barbershop, baby.

I've been told that in the barbershop, brothers discuss topics like women, sports betting, gifts, and personal accomplishments. My hubby tells me that they consider this "motion" aka anything these dudes or sisters have going on in their life. Now some of these tales may be lies or what I call bluffs. Men like to boost their egos often proving they are greater and improved than anyone else. Truth be told we all need each other, and that includes different genders. If not, why do you think God made us, all of us. I think he did so mostly so that we could learn while we are here on Earth and learn from one another. The barbershop may demonstrate some scoops of info much like the salon's dish "the tea." I imagine when the discussion is about women some of these conversations can get a bit rowdy just as the salon talk can get ratchet. Let's not stop there because a lot of good things also come out of the places. Barbershops are places where mentoring occurs and the sharing of various perspectives and what my husband likes to call group therapy. There are many youths and even men who may not have older father figures around them or in their lives. By going to these shops, they can glean from elders and peers and pick up knowledge they may not otherwise receive. Ro (the hubby) says shop talk often includes street life talks about how younger generations can avoid certain troubles. My son gave some insight on how being in the barbershop for men can be a peaceful area. I guess because there are no nagging women. It's just the men and boys with their cell phones other brothers and guy-talk. Many of the men there, by sharing their experiences, bond with other men and can learn skills, tips that may help them improve on themselves.

This is why in these spaces it is good that we come even if for just a few hours. It could mean a temporary escape from what you are dealing with in your personal life. You may even absorb some knowledge you can take back and apply for your own use. Sometimes, we can also come and get a renewal of our faith. You may have had this depending on where you go for your haircare services at least in a black salon. Community and faith are both important in Black culture. I know that for me haircare is self-care just like my husband feels barber care is group therapy. The faith of our ancestors Is often spoken of in these shops. We are also reminded of how God has been good to us over the years. The evidence is uncanny when we look back to a few short years ago and remember the past. Haircare for African American people was done in our homes over the sinks or in front of the hot stove. Black people would use lye and even straightening combs with hair grease in an attempt to make our hair more manageable. In the past we often had to huddle together in small groups of families because this is what was allowed. This was the time in which we could share our experiences, our suffering, and our faith. Today these places still exist to a degree. See what the Lord has done! I am mindful that all places of business for hair is not this way. In this day there are many ratchet things and people and in 2024 like this slang. The word ratchet was a derogatory word meant to put down a person but mostly directed towards females. I have read that it is a label for acting in an out-of-pocket manner. I do know in this culture and world of today there are many people who are too proud and out of character. They are even too proud to mention anything about God. This reminds me of a recent film festival where an actor displayed her dress with an image of Christ on the train and was pushed along all the way. Sister, we saw you represent and so did God. They want believers to pretend God doesn't exist and if you do keep quiet about him, it is also nonsense. We are taught in this world to respect other people's religions, right. Therefore, if you are offended that I represent Christ that is your business. Nevertheless, we must focus on the good things and strengthen the things that remain and that includes these sacred spaces.

When we allow ourselves to strip down all that burdens us and take a moment to breathe in fresh air and insight we are renewed. Visualize your next hair appointment as a time of internal self-care, cleaning and washing your hair and your spirit! When we take on the things of this world, we must return to God submitted and to be refreshed. One of my favorite services at the salon is washing my hair. I love to get shampoo and conditioner, deep conditioner, and every other treatment applied to my hair and then get my scalp rubbed and scrubbed. Baby, when you scrub my scalp, it just does something for me that causes me to utterly relax. To me this is an even better service than hair curling and styling. It's the wash for me! Sure, when my hair is done, I end up looking like a star. Shout-out to my stylist of many years who keeps me straight! In so many ways I feel good, and my self-esteem is good after this because I feel cleansed.

Going to church, praying, and getting to God does this for me spiritually. When I encounter the Holy Spirit, I feel refreshed, washed, cleaned. For a long time, I felt like having these encounters made me feel like a baby getting its hair washed by a loving parent. Today I feel something different when I have these encounters. What I feel after these moments is empowered and endowed to perform always on a higher plane, I feel resurrected. While we live in this world, we have the need to constantly be renewed. This is a weapon to help us fight back all the troubles and evil of this world. Just like my beauty salon helps me fight back this whatever number kinky hair. Yes, I said it so don't come for me. I will not pull back on this one. It doesn't just stop there. Every now and then you need a deep conditioning or a protein treatment or the guys may even get a clean shave or an edge line. I got something for all of these in the spirit don't you guys worry.

There are times in life where we are hurt or even feel like we've been cut so bad down to our soul and we need repair. God's love reaches deep down in us in these areas and does treatment. Things of the world try to attach themselves to us and make us uncomfortable much like a beard and to get free we must get clean. The Spirit cleans us like a fresh shave getting off all the stragglers. In the end we end up feeling pure and smooth just like a jaw or a baby's bottom. Going along in this fight of life we get tired and lose energy both physically and mentally and spiritually. Reading the Bible and meditating on your word and building yourself to learn more of it keep us sharp as a sword. Sharp like that white line some of the barbers at black hair shops put along these brothers' hairline to edge them up. Haircare, as you see now that we summarized above is important but Spiritual care is most important.

CHAPTER 29

WHEN WAS YOUR LAST "UGLY CRY"?

Crying is an emotional expression we humans release by shedding tears from our eyes. In doing this we are able to express emotion, be it pain or grief or some strong emotion that causes us to have an outburst. I have read that humans are the only creation that sheds emotional tears. To me this is a remarkably interesting thing. We were created so uniquely that our creator made this expression of emotion just for our race. He didn't give this to the animals to the plants or to even the angels, just us Humans. We must be special in God's system of creation.

We cry when we are sad but sometimes, we cry fueled by other emotions. Disappointment may cause one to cry or even anger. I, myself, cry at times when I made been mad. I grew to learn this happened when I bottled in my frustration and suppressed expressing my emotions. Now I manage how I cry more to some degree. What about kids? Children are known to cry out loud often. Perhaps because they may not be able to always vocalize what is wrong. There is a teachable moment in watching a child cry which we may be able to relate to. By allowing themselves to cry out there is a degree of stress relief, kids know how to expel and then they simply move on to something else.

When a child is crying adults adjust and sometimes may decide that it is no big deal. Now imagine the intensity and increase in volume when a kid ugly cries. I know you are just holding your breath waiting for me to explain what this is. Relax, breathe, no need for you fainting at this point in the book. Have you ever cried so hard and full of emotion that tears, snot seemed to well up from the innermost area of your soul? I have. This is the definition of an ugly cry. It is that desperate wailing type of cry you make when you feel like your very soul is being ripped away. Friends, this is not the normal type of crying. My guess is we each are allotted a handful of times when we experience an ugly cry. These are best used or produced sparingly and most people surrounding us don't know how they are to respond to this. The good news is that God is not troubled by our ugly cries. Nothing distresses God and he is not like us never overwhelmed never without power never surprised.

Being a child of God means he is already aware of all the experiences we will go through. All knowing God can comfort our grief, relieve our pain, and quell our anger. How do we get into these situations anyway? Easy, we live on Earth, and we are emotional beings. Truth is the innocent are quick to move on children who cry and then move on to something grow up into adult humans. Kids ugly cry all the time and they think nothing of it. For adults we just handle these things worse for some reason. Maturity often means we can't any longer just look over some of these things and move on, but we must stand firm and deal with things and solve problems.

I talked to my family about this, and they each gave me different perspectives. I drilled my kids and they each gave some great reasons for when we should ugly cry. One said it was appropriate to do so after a break-up in a relationship. The other said you may ugly cry after a bad argument with a best friend. My spouse inserted the death of a family member will cause you to ugly cry. He also stated finding out someone close is terminally ill could also cause this.

These are all good reasons to make you want to just let it all go. In my own experience besides the above listed reasons, I have ugly cried in times past due to my own reasons. When I missed a personal goal for myself I ugly cried. I was told I wouldn't graduate college with my incoming graduation class because I was short of a few credits due to my major. After finding out this I let out a big old ugly cry! Being delayed meant I let my family down but also, I let myself down. I forgot to tell you earlier I am competitive, and it is possible I kept that secretly concealed in my heart until now. Forgive me, this is a book I am coming clean in.

Years later I was diagnosed with CHF (congestive heart failure) after having my second child at just twenty-nine years old. Baby, this was my second time ugly crying and I felt distraught. I was just one-and-a-half years into a new marriage and warned due to my heart health and medications I would need not to have any more kids. Immediately I felt that I was a disappointment to my new husband, and it took me some weeks, months to get over this. Today I know a little more, that this disease runs in my family, and it is my intention to end it continuing with me.

In 2020 God shook the world and everything that could be shaken was. If you're not aware of what happened or not old enough to know it will be spoken of for many years to come. The world had a pandemic and like many households our house was affected. I lost my grandmother, my matriarch, due to COVID as she lived in a skilled nursing facility. She developed COVID after a new roommate was moved into her room from the hospital and she lived, and my grandmother died. My grandmother raised our family, and she lived in the house with my mom, my siblings and my father who after his first divorce moved in with us. I couldn't attend her funeral because she lived out of state in Georgia and so I had to view her funeral live online.

This was a jacked-up situation, and my heart goes out to all the families of the world who lost loved ones during the pandemic. My heart goes out to so many of you who couldn't be there or attend the funerals, or even celebrations of your loved ones. Many had similar situations to mine or worst and I pray for your comfort that God sends his Holy Spirit to heal you. In this same month my husband, the bread winner of the family was temporarily laid off. I was at the time a full-time health care worker and was under a great deal of stress as I worked in patient care. Every day I got up and forced myself to work being utterly burnt out, grieving, and depressed.

In hindsight, today all these situations were appropriate times for an ugly cry. People were stressed out like never before and I was one of them. Crying helped me to relieve some of the stress off me. After the crying I was able to change my course and pick back up my faith walk. There was a void after these situations and drinking wine wouldn't help, sex was temporary and sleeping in did nothing for financial issues. Somewhere in this situation I was met with an encounter from God. I don't remember if it was in a dream, if it was in a sermon, or during a possible alert from the Holy Spirit within, but I was reminded. I knew God, and I was reminded that he had a plan for me and that I was purposed for creating and all things artistic and couldn't just become stagnant but had to move forward.

I began to reach to do something new with my gifts and talents. I knew I could draw. I also used to fashion sketch, so I decided to pull out a sewing machine I bought and never used and learned via YouTube how to sew. Self-taught and all two-and-a-half years in now I know how to make clothes. Then I felt a need to develop other skills. I saw online how to create other things people did to bring extra money in during Covid and learned how to about an apply for my own business and I did. As I moved forward and kept developing new things to bring out of myself things turned around. My husband was called back by his company after being laid off for less than a few months and bought back full time with his benefits. Don't you tell me God isn't good. Today we have a YouTube Channel, a streetwear and Christian clothing line, and as you read, I am writing my first book.

I made an awesome discovery in this time that I could create like my God the Creator. Having two kids was no longer a disappointment, but I recognized the blessings God gifted me with. I have both a son and a daughter and am blessed to be able to impart wisdom, strength, and the love of God into both. With it being just two of them I can provide for them a better lifestyle and more choices than I ever had as a kid. Today I no longer look at delay in the same way. In my mind I keep a record of how my time is not God's timing. He makes everything beautiful in its season, me included. Things happen in life when they are supposed to.

For the time being if things are not going your way if you are in pain or only plain mad and you need to release have an ugly cry. Allow yourself a few of these moments in a lifetime to decompress. We are human for a reason and are meant to be able to shed emotions and this is ok! I like to tell my children when you are big angry or have a breakup or are grieving allow yourself a few hours or up to a full day to cry. Buy your Kleenex, blow your nose and let the tears drip down into your mouth. Who cares if you mess up your make-up or if your face turns red or your hair is a little disheveled afterwards. Cleanse your soul then eat a pint of your favorite ice cream and sulk but put a limit to your sorrow.

Ugly tears are cleansing tears. Let them go, friends! Just don't forget the next day is like day number one. Get up and wash your face then get dressed and look and do your best. Check in with God and get in sync to see where he next wants to lead you.

CHAPTER 30

SPEAK LIKE A COMMANDER

This chapter is for all my shy people. You must make changes in this day during this decade. People everywhere are sharing their opinion and their experiences all around us. Opinions exist everywhere and in every corner of the world wherever people live. I am drafting this book to capture the intention of the introverts and shy people out there at times I am one of you. I can be introverted at times, but I am no longer shy and not by a milestone. For the quiet, soft-spoken, and meek new friends I have out there, I have a word for you!

Today is a new day, and it's time for a new thing. by now you have heard the cliché I was today years old when I found out then you insert something at the end of this statement. I have found out you have to say what you need, and it must come from you. Open your mouth and use your words and be confident in your voice. I had to learn this as a life lesson myself. In my past I never felt like I was heard or taken seriously. To get to where I am now today, I had to grow. In my youth I detested being singled out and brought in front of a crowd of people to speak. I loved to sing when I was growing up but hated to be given the microphone at church because once again it led all eyes on me. It made me uncomfortable about my appearance but with time I realized it was me having a self-esteem issue.

Working with my cousin in her organization as a teen I was often given a microphone to speak in front of a platform and it helped me to learn my voice. She worked for a community development organization, and it helped families and children with services who otherwise couldn't afford them. One of the greatest things about this company, my older cousin and my father provided me on this Earth with exposure. For poor and middle-class children this means everything in their development. This is one reason why I am putting together my own non-profit organization to help minority girls with development services that will bridge them into becoming great in their futures. In high school and college these skills were developed as I was always selected and positioned to speak in front of a crowd. We were taught how to prepare our resumes, public speaking how to apply for internships even taken on college tours and taught etiquette lessons.

Friends, to become good at speaking in public, try to record yourself reading a page and listen and learn your voice. What do you sound like? Do you enunciate your words and are you articulate? You can build on these skills. Increase your vocabulary my own father helped me with this in childhood by forcing me to read encyclopedias. I know this dates me a little, but he also made me read newspapers daily. Today reading is one of my favorite hobbies. Next, I would say get in front of a mirror. Get used to seeing what you look like and love yourself. Keep doing this and you will slowly build your confidence. Then pick up a book and go ahead and read out loud while standing in front of the mirror. Today this is even easier thanks to our bougie cell phones and applications that let you read into a screen while recording a video and no one knows your reading.

My friend, the world needs you. If it were not the case, then you would not be here or still be here. There is not a person in this world who can be you. Not even if you were born a twin or of some other kind of multiple birth. Even in these cases there is something unique about each individual that God can single out. When you speak it is a collection of your personal thoughts, experiences, and your feelings. In the Bible we are taught by speaking you can even change your circumstances. This Bible demonstrated how God called things which were not as though they were. God the creator speaks to the result of a thing. This tells me that if we do not speak, we are left in situations that are just what we see when we could alter.

Speaking out loud then releases our faith. When we release our faith it's like re-patriated animals being released back into the wild. We free these animals in the act of changing the outcomes of their lives, species, and their existence. This is how our voices are heard. Try this exercise with me. No, I do not want pickles on my burger. I will not take the first slice of bread so you can have an inner slice. Do I look like a housekeeper? Do it yourself.

That my friends is liberating! It is important in life that you speak up and speak out. Otherwise, you will be given the leftovers and counted last. I know you are going to tell me that the Bible talks about the last being first, I know. It also talks about being the head and not the tail and you need to speak like you're the head. Where is your expectation may I ask? You've got to put on your big panties or boxers, respectively. Stop letting people of this world and your current situations "railroad" you. We have all been given a mouth and you must learn to use it. It may be the one of the reasons that God made it singular, so we don't come out of our faces more than we need to. There is nothing wrong with being mindful about how and what you say. Just know when you must say something and use your words, people.

Your voice is an instrument. It was given to you to uniquely imprint your word on this Earth and to worship God. Remember at one time Lucifer when he was an angle was given a voice unparallel to praise God with. The world needs you to speak what your peace of mind is. As children of God, we must demonstrate the same characteristics and power. You also were given your voice to praise and worship God as He deserves. We may not be able to hear it but creation I am sure in its own way gives thanks to God. Only us humans can relay it by voice of human words. Who can say that the animals, the trees and even the ocean and sky doesn't give praise to God. We just are not able to hear them do it. To be honest, are feeble human brains couldn't handle it because imagine hearing a squirrel or a tree or a rock crying out to God. Sending up prayers to him to give him thanks and us humans simply standing around and put to shame when we are the creatures that received a Spirit made after the image of God.

Then we have work to do, and it involves us letting our voices be heard. Be like a commander of your words. A commander is a leader whose job is to execute a mission. For the mission to be implemented a plan must first be spoken. Now you see this is the first most crucial step. First speak a word or a plan. Let's use the word grow. Next formulate a plan. Speak how it is that you grow and form a plan. Lastly put emphasis on your spoken word and endow it with strength, volume and finality. When you speak, you must mean what's said in absolute conviction without wavering or relenting but accomplishing your goal. Here is the final sample. I speak growth and I have a plan of steps and I know I will grow. Did you see how I used that word to build myself to form a goal and stand firm to complete with success.

A commander also has the job to hold power over his solders his terrain and to not give up territory. This is an important principal in our spiritual lives. Learning to use your voice is a necessary survival skill in your Christian journey. We must speak the Word of God to push back the plans of the enemy and to dismantle evil attempts and attacks. To do this, you must first learn the Word. Take time in your development by reading and studying the bible and becoming familiar with the teachings. Your voice is a spiritual weapon of defense. Just as it can be an instrument to praise God it can be a shield to dodge the fiery attacks of Satan. We must use our words and voice in the right way, or it can also cause detriment to us. It can cause you to fall if you speak wrong thoughts words or negatively. I love the scripture of the Bible that talks about the power of life and death lie in the tongue.

In times of the past, criminals would have their tongues cut out as a punishment. Without a tongue we can't even speak. In many ways this is a type of capital punishment because someone without a tongue can't say things that were not as though they are. If the criminal did reconsider, then God knows but they could never after this speak so out loud. Thankfully, God is not like man he knows our hearts.

At times in life, we may have a difficult walk or era where it is hard to speak as a commander. Things happen in life that distress and disheartens us like job loss, food insecurities, health concerns and other problems. During certain seasons at times in our lives it feels we are under attack this is known to the church community as spiritual warfare. It is real my friends and when it comes, you need some supernatural help to defeat and overcome it. If I could, like in my imagination, pull out my Samurai gear and sword and "go ham" (berserk) then I want to defend myself at this time. Then I learned that you can't fight a demonic attack or strongholds (thoughts) with physical strength. Physical strength I am good at, but spiritual strength was a weakness for me. At this point is when I felt like giving in the towel. Don't do it my friends. There is a strategy you must adopt for survival. WWCD this acronym is for what would a commander do. You must fight with your spiritual armor. You must put in the time and do the work to develop your spirit man to become a force. The Bible refers to it as the Armor of God.

Now God is pure and holy and without spot or blemish. I imagine this spiritual armor is a shiny white suit with decorations of fine gemstones and jewels much like the gates and city in Heaven is explained. This armor is without tarnish, it is impenetrable, it is heaven fashioned, and when I lead in prayer, it is given to me. I know this in my heart to be true. Christ who came into this world as our Jesus was a lamb without stain or blemish no sense. His power is infinite, and nothing will ever penetrate it or the rock that he is, my firm foundation. My friends, you now have the gift that keeps on giving. The armor of God is the gift and Jesus is the rock that we can stand on. God the Father our Creator is our shield, and the Holy Spirit is our breast plate our covering that keeps us in right relations with God.

Finally, a commander speaks a charge out to his soldiers. God is my commander and he commanded us to go! Go out to all nations all people and in every corner of the Earth to teach about Jesus his sacrifice for us and redemption to God. I may not be behind a pulpit teaching it. You may see this in me when you purchase some of the merch I am selling. You may experience God in reading this book that I wrote. You may laugh at my crazy YouTube channels or find me on the streets here somewhere in Florida. My hope though is that when you encounter me that you encounter God. God is inside of me and if you open your heart he will come in and live inside of you too. You just may have to get through all my crazy first. Love God and have fun in this world. Don't forget to pray and help someone else. Give and share your testimony to someone. Spend your time, talents, gifts, money, and your energy while you are here in this world. Give everything you can in this life journey until you are empty. When all is done and you have completed your assignment, rest well.

EPILOGUE

First, I am so proud of you all for hanging in there to this final page with me. Give yourself a clap because we are friends now. Like me, you are persistent and relentless at the same time. For some this might be an easy read and I want to acknowledge all the authors out there drafting a book is tougher than it looks. I started out by handwriting some "chicken-scratch" on a few pages, but it looked more like journaling, and I am glad you didn't see my handwriting. It's bad, people, trust me.

The beginning of this book was easy because I had prewritten about a total of sixty pages back and front on paper, so I was like this is going to be a breeze. Honey, think again. After that, I fattened up what was previously written like I fattened this stomach over the last two years, but I digress. I finally fell flat. Now I know what it is like to experience writer's block. I was gifted a shiny new laptop last Christmas, and I vowed that right after the new year I would take to typing away at this book until I get to the end. Sounds good.

I landed into a period of about one month in which I purposely avoided writing and indulged on that bottle of wine or few glasses and deferred the book completion. I went out for nice dinners and created content online and did much preparation to launch an online store. This book though kept being put on the back burner. It was stifling being at this point and I was stagnant and then I had a revelation. Some years ago, more than a decade, I learned about creating a one-year, five-year, and ten-year goal plan for myself. As for the annual goals, I update them every year and put a calendar on my bedroom wall to remind me of them. I set a goal in each month of the year to complete something I wish to accomplish. As I got out of bed one morning and looked up, I saw it dead in my face. Author a book and finish and publish it by my birthday in May. I started creating this work in August of 2023 and in just under ten months I am on my way to edit and publish. I have never authored a book before but if other people could do it, then I couldn't imagine why I couldn't. I am articulate I think and creative and more importantly I told you I like to delve into many different projects at a time. I love options.

Thank you for reading this book. I hope you enjoyed it because I did make it. Ok, not the writer's block part but after I did.

Don't be afraid to accept God because of what other people think. Dive into your Christian journey and don't be stiff.

Laugh and have fun often, life is full of enough sadness and tears.

Oh, and if you happen to meet me on the streets, say "hi."

ACKNOWLEDGEMENTS

I first have to say I couldn't do any of this without God. This book has been a hot mess since my sudden thoughts in 2023. An idea came to me of suddenly becoming an author after hearing a sermon on how I can be more than one thing. With some commitment the mess seemed to have taken shape and come together. In many ways this is like our lives prior to accepting salvation in Christ. In this my first book I would like to give thanks to my family for enduring with me. I picked their brains constantly asking for synonyms and brainstormed with them on some of my chapter topics and for that I am grateful.

To my siblings I love you even from a different state and our lives are better today because of the experiences we shared from the past. My big sister, who when I shared this told me she was also drafting a book, I can't wait to read it because you are full of mischievousness, and I can only imagine the stories your book will have in it.

To my hubby, my best friend, my chocolate drop, and my silly partner, I love you. God somehow put us both together which makes for twice the amount of laughter being we are both silly. I thank you for your support in everything and for encouraging me to live my dreams and to continually expand on new ones.

My God, you are the greatest. I can't imagine my life without you. I have been saved so many times by you and every day, month, and year I want to be a little closer to your throne.

I didn't forget about the readers and fans. Sharing my laughter and joy is better with you. I wish you much joy and success in your lives. In the end I don't want to go to Hell! I hope this book helps you to save your soul, find encouragement, and renews your faith so you won't go either. Buy a book and then get a second copy for a family member or a friend. Don't leave me out here by myself we all need to Kiss Our Cross. Besides, there are worse things out here you could be kissing. Ok, just playing again, see you soon.

NOTES

1. Chesire Cat, from Alice in Wonderland by Lewis Caroll 1865.

2. Tommy shirt also known as Tommy Hilfiger Polo Shirt 1998.

3. David danced before the Lord 2 Samuel 6:14-22

4. "Everything happens for a reason" Aristotle.

5. Dr. Phillip W. Archer former Biology Dean at Virginia Union University

6. "Why by the cow when you can get the Milk for free unknown author,18th century England.

7. Dora the Explorer Doll Jumbo size Mattel 2003.

8. Boxing like iron Mike as in the Mike Tyson Heavyweight Champion 1986.

9. "Smite almighty Smiter" Bruce the Almighty Movie May 2003.

10. "It was the best of times, it was the worst of times", Charles Dickens A Tale of Two Cities.

11. "Who the son sets free, is free indeed.", John 8:36.

12. "Deez Nuts", comedian Welven Da Great of Instagram 2015.

13. Lego-The Master Builder Movie 2014.

14. "The gag is,", Keke Palmer 2016 on Late Night Show.

15. "When they go low, we go to Hell," Unknown manager.

16. ike Mayweather as in professional boxing champion Floyd Mayweather. Jr.

17. Job chapter 38, The Holy Bible

18. Pac-Man video game May 1980 creator Toro Iwatani.

19. Tabitha Brown, Actor, Emmy Host, Author, Social Media Personality.

20. Apostle Paul, Romans 7:21, Holy Bible

21. Ratchet as defined by The Urban Dictionary February 2023.

ABOUT THE AUTHOR

LYNETTE S. DUROCHER is a businessperson, author, healthcare worker, and social media content creator. Alongside her husband she founded Stella Ro, LLC, a clothing apparel platform for Christian and Classic Car Streetwear.

Lynette is a mom to two children, Trin and E.J, and resides in Florida. Alongside her husband Ro they have developed this business to save lost souls to encourage and build faith in Christians and non-believers. They have two active brands including Brown Sugar for classic car enthusiasts and smack talk and Abide for Christian streetwear and soon to include novels, ready-to-wear clothing and kitchenware. As for he and her house they will abide in the secret place of the Most-High God.

Hope to see you soon!

www.ingramcontent.com/pod-product-compliance
Lightning Source LLC
Chambersburg PA
CBHW020405130626
46549CB00006B/2444